T0291318

Johannessen's book is a gripping read. His rich, critical, and lucid account is grounded in world events and the socio-political exigencies and rationales that drove complexity ideas first in one direction and then another. The scope of the book is both broad and deep, drawing as it does on a range of disciplines including physics, biology, sociology, psychology, history, and philosophy. His writing is exceptionally clear, accessible, and jargon-free, which is no small achievement given the subject matter of the book.

Farhad Dalal, *PhD, Psychotherapist and Group Analyst, Devon, UK.*

The book is a compelling demonstration of how traditional views on organizations and management throughout the recent century have fallen short of their promise to control the evolution and complexity of organizations and society. Consequently, in facing complexity there is an acute and fundamental need to reframe our views on organizations, society, and management.

Thijs Homan, *Professor and Consultant on Organizational Change, Netherlands.*

Johannessen provides clear routes through the terrain of different intellectual traditions of complexity. The book is written with clarity, care for detail, and a pace that is all too absent on the academic bookshelf. The strength of this unique exploration is that it enables readers to explore the ideas that loosely hold the field together and to venture into areas that we might be less familiar with.

Rob Warwick, *Professor of Management and Organizational Learning, Business School, University of Chichester, UK.*

This concise book succeeds in providing an overview of the growth of complexity theory and its applications, showing the significance of this framework for the theory and practice of organizations and leadership. It is a lucid book, useful as a manual, enlightening as a textbook, and thought-provoking as a contribution to a vibrant intellectual field.

Thomas Hylland Eriksen, *Professor of Social Anthropology, University of Oslo, Norway.*

The book is a concise and accessible guide to the field of complexity sciences in the organizational context, expertly and constructively covering both the foundations and the enduring tensions between the various complexity theories. I strongly recommend the book as an essential research overview for students and more advanced scholars alike.

Harri Raisio, *Senior Lecturer, Complexity Research Group,*
University of Vaasa, Finland.

Complexity is an acutely important theme on the agenda of today's leaders and organizational actors. This book is an excellent insight into how theories of complexity have evolved in the tension between the natural sciences and the human sciences, and how key researchers have developed ideas of complexity in the political contexts of their time.

Tor Olav Grøtan, *PhD, Senior Research Scientist, SINTEF DIGITAL, and*
Associate Professor, Norwegian University of Science and Technology, Norway.

In this book the reader gets new perspectives on organizations, perspectives that embrace complexity rather than simplify the theme. Johannessen's approach demonstrates the diversity of perspectives on complexity in organizations and triggers new questions. The book will certainly be useful for students and scholars as a guide to the development of new knowledge in future organization and management research.

Fredrik Nilsson, *Professor, Department of Design Sciences,*
Lund University, Sweden.

Complexity in Organizations

Written with pace and clarity, this book is a comprehensive and compact overview and introduction to the research landscape of complexity in organizations.

In addition to conveying a gripping history of how complexity has influenced organizational ideas, theories, and practices throughout the 20th century and into our present age, the book sheds light on how groundbreaking ideas in chaos and complexity research have emerged and challenged the very foundations of science into a changed vision of nature, society, and human organizations. As well as being an exciting investigation into complexity research in organizations, the book shows how, in the past, researchers who were immersed in the power politics of their day grappled with the theme of complexity in their quest to understand the dynamics of organization in nature and society. By welding fundamental theoretical themes and practical implications into the political and social contexts in which they emerged, this overview provides both depth and breadth to the history, as well as the future, of studies of complexity in organized activity.

The book is a lucid and essential study of a topic that will be of interest to scholars, researchers, and students in the fields of business and management, especially those with an interest in the ways that complexity affects and transforms organizations.

Stig O. Johannessen is Professor of Organization and Leadership at Nord University and Oslo Metropolitan University, Norway.

State of the Art in Business Research
Series Editor: Geoffrey Wood

Recent advances in theory, methods and applied knowledge (alongside structural changes in the global economic ecosystem) have presented researchers with challenges in seeking to stay abreast of their fields and navigate new scholarly terrains.

State of the Art in Business Research presents shortform books which provide an expert map to guide readers through new and rapidly evolving areas of research. Each title will provide an overview of the area, a guide to the key literature and theories and time-saving summaries of how theory interacts with practice.

As a collection, these books provide a library of theoretical and conceptual insights, and exposure to novel research tools and applied knowledge, that aid and facilitate in defining the state of the art, as a foundation stone for a new generation of research.

Remote Working
A Research Overview
Alan Felstead

Business History
A Research Overview
John F. Wilson, Ian G. Jones, Steven Toms, Anna Tilba, Emily Buchnea and Nicholas Wong

Complexity in Organizations
A Research Overview
Stig O. Johannessen

For more information about this series, please visit: www.routledge.com/State-of-the-Art-in-Business-Research/book-series/START

Complexity in Organizations
A Research Overview

Stig O. Johannessen

Routledge
Taylor & Francis Group

LONDON AND NEW YORK

First published 2022
by Routledge
4 Park Square, Milton Park, Abingdon, Oxon OX14 4RN

and by Routledge
605 Third Avenue, New York, NY 10158

Routledge is an imprint of the Taylor & Francis Group, an informa business

© 2022 Stig O. Johannessen

The right of Stig O. Johannessen to be identified as author of this work
has been asserted in accordance with sections 77 and 78 of the Copyright,
Designs and Patents Act 1988.

British Library Cataloguing-in-Publication Data
A catalogue record for this book is available from the British Library

Library of Congress Cataloging-in-Publication Data
Names: Johannessen, Stig O., author.
Title: Complexity in organizations: a research overview /
    Stig O. Johannessen.
Description: Milton Park, Abingdon, Oxon; New York, NY: Routledge,
    2022. | Includes bibliographical references and index.
Identifiers: LCCN 2021057916 (print) | LCCN 2021057917 (ebook) |
    ISBN 9780367860189 (hardback) | ISBN 9781032271644 (paperback) |
    ISBN 9781003042501 (ebook)
Subjects: LCSH: Organization. | Management.
Classification: LCC HD31.2 .J64 2022 (print) | LCC HD31.2 (ebook) |
    DDC 658.4—dc23/eng/20211209
LC record available at https://lccn.loc.gov/2021057916
LC ebook record available at https://lccn.loc.gov/2021057917

ISBN: 978-0-367-86018-9 (hbk)
ISBN: 978-1-032-27164-4 (pbk)
ISBN: 978-1-003-04250-1 (ebk)

DOI: 10.4324/9781003042501

Typeset in Times New Roman
by Apex CoVantage, LLC

Contents

Acknowledgements

Over the past two decades, I have had the pleasure of engaging with students, colleagues, and leaders in many interesting discussions on the implications of complexity thinking. These conversations have been highly valuable and important for my understanding of complexity in organizations. I wish to express my great appreciation to each and every one who has contributed to my learning experience and my research over the years.

In the present project, I wish to thank the peer reviewers who provided very helpful comments on the ideas and draft versions of this book. My thanks are also owed to Catriona Turner for English-language advice. Many thanks are given to Senior Publisher Terry Clague and his team at Routledge for their highly professional guidance and support. I extend my warmest thanks and appreciations to my wonderful family for their enduring patience and encouragements.

Trondheim, Norway, February 2022
Stig O. Johannessen

About the Author

Stig O. Johannessen is Professor of Organization and Leadership at the Faculty of Social Sciences at Nord University and the Department of Behavioural Science at Oslo Metropolitan University, Norway. He holds an MSc in Physics and a PhD in Industrial Economics and Technology Management from the Norwegian University of Science and Technology. His research explores complexity in the interaction space between natural sciences, social sciences, and philosophy, and the way complexity thinking can help people in business and society to adapt and create when faced with 'wicked problems' and crises. Professor Johannessen has been visiting scholar at universities in Europe, United States, and Australia, and he is working with major private and public organizations on issues of strategic leadership and decision-making in contexts of complexity and crisis. He is the author/co-author and editor/co-editor of more than 100 academic and popular publications, including 12 books, among them *Strategy, Leadership and Complexity in Crisis and Emergency Operations* and the four-volume reference work *Complexity in Organizations*.

Introduction – Complexity in Organizations

Complexity in organizations is far from a coherent research field constrained to a particular scientific discipline. As a research theme concerning the change and stability of organized activity – whether in nature or society – complexity has rather emerged from a multitude of sources and disciplines over a period of time dating at least back to the 19th century. In the literature on organizational studies, the theme of complexity first became visible in the wake of World War II, when researchers raised criticism against the mechanical view of people and organizations that had been dominating during the rise of industrialization in the 19th and early 20th centuries.

However, even though complexity emerged as a post-war theme in society and organizations, no specific complexity theory of organizations was developed until the 1990s.

Since then, studies of the relevance of complexity theories to organizations have been conducted in various research fields aiming at understanding the dynamics of organized activity (for comprehensive overviews of the research fields, see Allen et al., 2011; Johannessen and Kuhn, 2012).

The purpose of this book is to offer an introductory overview of how complexity has been treated as a theme in organizational studies since the late 1940s and especially since the 1990s. The book draws on seminal texts, articles, and books that are often referred to in the research literature on complexity in organizations. Additionally, research is included from a range of sources that are directly or indirectly relevant to the background and context of the specific organizational research literature.

Thus, the book reflects the most important and influential ideas, which in various ways have stimulated and underpinned the research theme of complexity in organizations from a diversity of disciplines over several decades. By encompassing the historical aspects of the book's theme, light is shed on the societal, political, and academic contexts in which the key researchers have operated and their ideas forged, discussed, popularized, accepted, or rejected. The book is divided into two parts, each with four chapters, which in turn are subdivided according to key themes.

Foundations of Complexity in Organizational Theories

Part 1 focuses on the origins of complexity as a theoretical theme in organizations. This part of the book adopts a historical approach, primarily to provide readers who are not acquainted with the origins of complexity ideas with some of the connections between otherwise seemingly unrelated fields. Collectively, the four chapters in Part 1 endeavour to lay out how complexity came to be a theme in organizational studies and how it has been treated in various streams of organization theory.

Chapter 1 presents the attempts to deal with complexity in organizations in the first half of the 20th century in the context of the political and social environment in which the ideas of key thinkers emerged and spread. The chapter covers how theories about systems in the natural sciences were exported to organization theory and became part of an ideological unification of the sciences under the flag of a general systems theory. As complexity became integrated into a cross-disciplinary systems' understanding directed at bridging the natural and human sciences, it also became a theme in organizational studies.

Chapter 2 demonstrates how, during the 1940s and early 1950s, the technological idea of organizations from early in the history of industrialization was upgraded in concert with a new view of complexity in organizations. The mechanistic view of organizations was reshaped as *cybernetics* – the science of feedback control.

Cybernetics inspired new branches within the human sciences, such as cognitivist psychology, as researchers started to attend to motivational needs, as well as to the development of people and groups in organizations. During the post-war decades, there was an emerging shift towards the importance of human relations and group identity, and the mobilization of people's intellectual and social abilities to collaborate in groups. However, the rise of computers and cybernetics also meant a revival of a machine view of humans, aimed at reducing and controlling complexity in organizations.

Chapter 3 reviews some of the developments within systems theories and their take on complexity in organizations from the1950s to the 1980s. Systems theories evolved within a range of social scientific disciplinary approaches to organizational studies, including economics, psychology, political science, sociology, and cultural studies. However, systems theories did not offer any progress in the foundation of organizational theory with regard to complexity.

Chapter 4 points to the origins and development of complexity theories in the natural sciences, engineering, and organizations. First, there were advancements within *non-equilibrium thermodynamics*, from its theoretical breakthrough in the early 1930s to the theories of self-organizing dissipative structures in the 1960s and 1970s. Second, there was the interest in *non-linear dynamics* in mathematics, which gained momentum as a result of the need to solve engineering problems related to space flights. And finally, there was the discovery in meteorology that weather dynamics can be described in terms of *chaos theory*. Combined, these developments created a new view of complexity in the natural sciences, a view that from the late 1980s came to be bundled together under the term *complexity sciences*, and through popular literature attracted the attention of organizational researchers and managers, and inspired a new generation of distinctive theoretical approaches to organizations in the late 20th century.

During the 1990s, the ideas from complexity research in the natural sciences created new directions in organizational studies of complexity. Although the basic concepts and ideas seemed coherent originally, by the turn of the millennium researchers had developed a greater diversity of complexity theories in organizations and their relation to the philosophical basis in the natural sciences and the human sciences.

Philosophy, Science, and Organizational Practice

Studies of complexity are shaped by the full spectrum of ideals and philosophies in the human sciences and natural sciences. Therefore, it is important not only to discuss the relationships and interactions between the different sciences but also to explore the potential of such dynamics with regard to complexity theories in organizational studies.

In Part 2 of the book, the chapters encourage awareness of the philosophical issues and assumptions of bridging the sciences in researching complexity in organizations. Additionally, it outlines some of the key insights from applied research. Understanding complexity in organizations requires crossing traditional boundaries between the sciences and their associated world views. There are different research traditions, ideals, and practices in the various disciplines, sub-disciplines, and cross-disciplinary fields in different sciences. The implications and applications of complexity thinking have become interpreted and disseminated in an array of issues and organizational research fields. Within organizational studies, specific topics include complexity ideas of organizational practice, strategy and organizational dynamics, as well as leadership, organizational change, and innovation.

Chapter 5 presents some of the philosophical and methodological tensions arising in the discussion of research on complexity in organizations. As complexity ideas originated in the natural sciences, a critical view must be taken on the discussion of what the ideas mean when imported into social and organizational studies. The philosophical and methodological discussion of the problems of the two sciences versus a unified science is an important part of the groundwork for research on complexity in organizations.

The chapter explores how American pragmatists introduced a philosophy that bears resemblance to ideas of complexity in human action. Pragmatism was at odds with classical social sciences, a debate that peaked in the 1930s but dwindled in the wake of World War II. In subsequent decades, social science and organizational studies favoured unification and synthesis of social theory in structuralist schools, while the pragmatist alternative remained in the dark.

From the 1980s onwards, a renewed interest in philosophical pragmatism emerged in both German and American philosophy as a result of debates between Jürgen Habermas and Niklas Luhmann in Germany, and Richard Rorty and Hilary Putnam in the United States. The development coincided with the emergence of theories of chaos and complexity in organizational studies, although the potential of bringing the ideas together was not explored.

Chapter 6 explores the possibilities in organizational theory and complexity yet further by bringing together ideas from complexity research with recent developments in philosophy and social theory. Since the turn of the millennium, particular interest has emerged in merging chaos and complexity ideas with what broadly could be termed two directions – one based in postmodern philosophies and one in pragmatist philosophies. On this basis, an argument is developed in the chapter regarding a possible way forward towards a coherent understanding of complexity in organizations. New insights might be found in the exploration of human experience in terms of fundamental processes of time, space, and rhythm.

Human experiences are constructed from repetition, fluctuations, and differences in interactional patterns. Taking account of the complexity is to adhere to the movement and rhythm of such human experience as an approach to understanding the stabilization and change of everyday practices. Thus, a shift is suggested from seeing organizations as physical and static objects (systems) towards seeing technologies and social structures in terms of past enactments in temporal horizons of time and space – processes whereby the premises for future events and actions are entangled with the experiences of what has gone before. In these processes, humans organize themselves and their environments. The argument underlines that an interpretation of the phenomena of emergence and self-organization as expressions of crisis is of particular importance in human experiences of communication, power, identity, and ethics, all of which are interactional phenomena that fuel the emergence, dissipation, stabilization, and collapse of organized human activity.

Chapter 7 discusses the implications and applications of complexity ideas with regard to strategy and organizational dynamics, themes which are inevitably guided by questions concerning how organizations are sustained and changed over time. Embedded in such approaches is a set of assumptions about people's capacity to predict and know the future with any degree of certainty. As this capacity is very limited, it can be expected that researchers who are working from a base in complexity thinking are interested in how human organized activity adapts and co-evolves when the future is uncertain, as well as what role and relations the individual actor has in this regard. Thus, attention is focused on assumptions about specific issues of complexity dynamics, such as time, emergence, and self-organization, and particularly what this means in human terms.

Chapter 8 continues to explore the implications and applications of organizational complexity ideas, focusing on leadership and organizational change. From different avenues of complexity research, the call for new ways of understanding and practising leadership includes being attentive to emerging trends and the self-organizing processes of social reality. Leaders and their consultants are often tasked with working out programmes of change in organizations. At the same time, such programmes often refer to change as a hierarchical phenomenon – something that is happening either as a top-down or as a bottom-up process. To work differently with change when inspired by complexity ideas implies redefining what hierarchy means and thereby redefining the practice of leadership. The chapter focuses attention on a particularly popular aspect of change in organizations, namely innovation, which refers to how a new product, service, or organizational practice emerges. Innovation has been explored with reference to metaphors from chaos and complexity research, such as self-organizing emergence of dissipative structures. However, framing innovation processes within the social theoretical ideas of complexity implies that innovation processes are highlighted as communicative processes wherein power, identity, and ethics are challenged and potentially changed.

Throughout this book, the various facts and discussions from complexity research are placed in context. The focus is on not only what complexity researchers in organizational studies agree on but also how they differ in their thinking, what their inspirations are, and how they have positioned themselves in relation to philosophical discussions. In this way, the book is intended to serve as a platform for further studies on the theme of complexity in organizations. Each chapter includes a list of references that should provide readers with an opportunity to pursue such further studies.

The book is intended for students and researchers who are interested in how complexity has inspired a dialogue between the natural sciences, social sciences, and philosophy. It could be seen as aiding in building an understanding of how research and thinking about complexity in organizations have been an integral part of the knowledge of organizations for at least a century. First, complexity was seen as a problem to be removed, then it was approached as a challenge that could be handled and contained, and recently complexity has found specific grounds in a number of academic and organizational fields as an inevitable and integrated aspect of human reality.

Currently, there are many possible new research questions and topics to be explored concerning complexity and organizations, ranging from philosophical and theoretical foundations to understanding the dynamics of concrete organizational and societal realities. Given our highly dynamic and interactional world, in which humans, technology, and nature are entangled together in time, space, and a common destiny, exploring complexity demands overcoming a rationale of splitting reality into scientific disciplines. Investigating complexity is tantamount to exploring the interactional, dynamic, and integrative aspects of human and natural reality. Thus, there is every reason to believe that as a research theme complexity will continue to be crucial for our understanding of the dynamics of organizations and societies.

References

Allen, P., Maguire, S. & McKelvey, B. (eds.) (2011). *The SAGE Handbook of Complexity and Management*. London: SAGE.

Johannessen, S.O. & Kuhn, L. (eds.) (2012). *Complexity in Organization Studies*. Four-volume set. London: SAGE.

Part 1

Foundations of Complexity in Organizational Theories

1 Early Attempts to Deal With Complexity in Organizations

Reducing Complexity: Organizations as Machines

Throughout the rise of industrialization in the 19th and early 20th centuries, a mechanical view of organizations became influential in the management of factories where people worked alongside machines to mass-produce products in a tightly disciplined production scheme, which the American engineer Frederick Winslow Taylor called *scientific management* (Taylor, 1911). The reference to management as being scientific was akin to treating people in the same way as if they were cogwheels in the machines that engineers had constructed for the purpose of speeding up the rate of standardized production.

In his book on scientific management, Taylor proposed a solution to the problem of motivating workers to maximize their performance: what if people were paid according to their productivity? The more efficient and faster the work was carried out, the more they would earn. This solution would motivate workers to work harder for extra income, while the capital owner would benefit from higher returns on capital because more products would be sold. Faced with some sense of complexity, which he called 'complicated', Taylor thought everyone would benefit from his idea:

> In the case of a more complicated manufacturing establishment, it should also be perfectly clear that the greatest permanent prosperity for the workman, coupled with the greatest prosperity for the employer, can be brought about only when the work of the establishment is done with the smallest combined expenditure of human effort, plus nature's resources, plus the cost for the use of capital in the shape of machines, buildings, etc. Or, to state the same thing in a different way: that the greatest prosperity can exist only as the result of the greatest possible productivity of the men and machines of the establishment – that is, when each man and machine is turning out the largest possible output.
> (Taylor, 1911, p. 11)

DOI: 10.4324/9781003042501-2

Taylor provided evidence in support of his theory by referring to several companies in which his way of thinking about production had been implemented. The implementation had resulted in them 'earning large dividends and at the same time paying from 30% to 100% higher wages to their men than are paid to similar men immediately around them, and with whose employers they are in competition' (ibid., p. 11).

Taylor's idea was implemented in the Ford factories and in many other industrial companies, and it became the preferred industrial management ideology in the first decades of the 20th century, to the extent that to this day it is known as *Taylorism*. The success of the ideology was based upon certain technologies and inventions such as the assembly line. Measurement and reduction of time spent on working tasks were introduced to enable precise calculations of the payment made to each worker. In an expanding consumer market, the main focus of factory managers was on maximizing production capacity through internal efficiency and productivity in order to meet the growing demands for their products.

Taylorism dealt with complexity by trying to remove or reduce it. Specifically, efforts were directed towards removing or reducing human complexity, organizational complexity, and technological complexity. Its instrumental essence (i.e. the division of work into the smallest operations and payment according to productivity) was about avoiding the natural flexibility and creativity of people by treating and 'oiling' them in the same way as machine parts. This raised the following problems: What about those workers who worked just as hard as others but were unable to produce the same results? What about those who became sick or were injured at the workplace? What about those who suffered psychological depression due to their monotonous work? Attention paid to the dehumanizing aspects of Taylorism slowly stirred some counterarguments towards the form of work that had become normal in factories, counterarguments that grew into a movement that became known as the *human relations movement* (Likert, 1947; Trist and Bamforth, 1951; Bruce, 2006).

Awareness of Complexity: The Importance of Human Relations

The human relations movement directed attention towards the psychological and social aspects of working life. Productivity and motivation seemed to be linked not only to the payment according to performance but also to the social working environment, as revealed by the well-known Hawthorne studies (Mayo, 1933, 1949; Roethlisberger and Dickson, 1939), a series of studies that were carried out in the second half of the 1920s at Western Electric's plants, just outside Hawthorne, Illinois, USA. With the insight that people can be motivated and productive when given the opportunity to take responsibility in a work group, a new philosophy of leadership was also emerging, a philosophy that could be traced back to Mary Parker Follett's ideas of democratic leadership (Follett, 1923, 1926). Although the early promoters of human relations in organizations did not explicitly introduce theories of complexity in organizations, an awareness of the theme of complexity as a positive aspect of life in organizations was emerging. However, before the humanistic ideology got the chance to take hold, the world was thrown into a different and more destructive route.

Destruction of Human Complexity: World War II

World War II represented a great paradox: on the one hand, it was the pinnacle of the implementation of ideas about removing human complexity and diversity, while, on the other hand, it took a great deal of mobilization of human cooperation and ingenuity to end it. The war demonstrated an unprecedented reduction and destruction of humanity first and foremost by the German Nazi state's industrial-scale organization of mass murder during the Holocaust. Moreover, state-organized mass murder of civilians, justified by ideology, had also taken place just before the war – during the 1930s in Stalin's Soviet Union. In Asia, the Japanese actively used mass murder as a way of implementing ethnic superiority and nationalistic ideology during their expansion into China and elsewhere from 1937. Also, on the side of allied countries fighting against Germany and Japan, mass killings of civilians were justified as a means to end the war. Hundreds of thousands of civilians were killed in the destruction of German cities such as Dresden by the Allied powers' carpet bombings, the United States' firebombing air raids of Tokyo, and the dropping of atomic bombs on the Japanese cities of Hiroshima and Nagasaki during the final stages of the war. It all testified to the scale of the brutality exercised by military forces from democratic nations. By the end of the war, it had become painfully clear that the era of science, rationalism, and human enlightenment, which since the 17th century had influenced the Western world, had ended in a total collapse of humanity to the point of self-annihilation.

Dealing With Complexity: Unifying Science, Technology, and Politics

The world's emergence from the ruins of World War II was accompanied by a widespread hope of building a more humane world, one with respect for individual rights and social coexistence. The establishment of the United Nations on 24 October 1945 testifies to that coherent hope for humanity and peace around the world. Rebuilding a world based on universal human values would mean not only a new notion of human complexity but also dealing with social, political, organizational, and technological complexity in new ways.

Thus, World War II was a crucial dividing period in history when it comes to organizational studies, in general, and for complexity as a theme in such studies, in particular. The time had come for organizations to learn not from the cold efficiency of machines, as Taylor had proposed, but from the synthesis of life itself – from biology and living nature, where higher levels of order are created in dynamic tension between stability and renewal. Synthesis and harmonic order, not reductionism and polarization, seemed to be the way forward. This new organizational ideology was to become important, as it blended into a new spirit in Western post–World War II societies.

However, the new approach had to take account of technology, which had progressed during the war and had laid the foundation for rocket science, computers, and electronics. The British mathematician Alan Turing's first design for a stored-program computer was published in 1946 (Copeland, 2004), after he had worked on code-breaking machines during the war. The first programmable digital computer, Electronic Numerical Integrator and Computer (ENIAC)), was ready in the United States in late 1945, while the transistor, which enabled the construction of smaller electronic devices, was invented in 1947. Technology was moving away from the early period of mechanical machines towards a new period of electronic and digital technology. The shift also required new ways of thinking about organizations.

In their effort to embrace and to control complexity and technology, researchers in the natural sciences, social sciences, engineering, economy, and philosophy took interest in cross-disciplinary themes and critiques of established views in science, society, and organizations. As researchers and leaders were trying to wrap their minds around the integrated dynamics and evolution of the new world of science, technology, politics, society, and work organizations, they started to embrace ideas of collaboration in multidisciplinary and cross-disciplinary work teams to solve complex problems.

In 1948, in an article titled 'Science and complexity', the American science administrator Warren Weaver wrote about the development. He thought science and society could progress to solve problems of complexity if science projects and production were organized in multidisciplinary teams supported by computers that could provide operational decision support, just like they did during the war:

> In addition to the general growing evidence that problems of organized complexity can be successfully treated, there are at least two promising

bits of special evidence. Out of the wickedness of war have come two new developments that may well be of major importance in helping science to solve these complex twentieth-century problems. The first piece of evidence is the wartime development of new types of electronic computing devices. . . . The second of the wartime advances is the 'mixed-team' approach of operations analysis.

(Weaver, 1948, p. 6)

However, at the time it was not only the harmonious chorus of humanity and collaboration that was heard. Another, much colder and disharmonious tune played in the background as the prospect of a different kind of war was threatening, a war that would be infinitely more terrifying and destructive than any previous wars. With the dropping of the atomic bombs on Hiroshima and Nagasaki, the United States had introduced the possibility of a nuclear war. A new type of competition gave impetus to ideas in science and technology, one that at the same time was deeply integrated with global power politics: the nuclear arms race and its 'Siamese twin', the race for space.

In the context and associated atmosphere of the threat of nuclear war, it would seem impossible to base Western society and organizations on only one of the two contrasting and competing organizational management ideas: the technological instrumentalism of Taylorism or the psychological approach of the human relations movement. Technology without human ethics would lead the world to destruction. Humanity without technology, meaning the West not engaging in the technological competition with the Soviet Union, would risk the Western democracies becoming technologically and military inferior to an expanding totalitarian communist regime.

Understanding how organized complexity, as Weaver termed it, could be dealt with, stimulated a cross-disciplinary interest in research on the fusion of knowledge about living nature, technology, and organizations based on generalized frameworks of science and society. The idea of a *unity* of the natural sciences and the human sciences had a strong ideological flavour, and it was to frame organizational reality in terms of a biological metaphor of holistic systems combined with the idea of self-regulating technological systems.

Thus, the theme of complexity became visible in organizational research from the 1950s as part of the rise of a dualistic idea that organizations must be seen as systems: on the one hand, as complex, dynamic, and open to fluxes of energy and matter in the same way as living organisms (Bertalanffy, 1950a) and, on the other hand, as regulated and controlled, much like thermostats and other technological control systems (Wiener, 1948). On that basis, theories of organization and management synthesized human and technological ideas in the form of *general systems theory* (Boulding, 1956), *socio-technical systems theory* (Emery and Trist, 1960), *systems dynamics* (Forrester, 1961), and *open systems theory* (Katz and Kahn, 1966). From the mid-1960s, these theories gradually became dominant in analyses and understandings of organizations. Accordingly, based on the same theories, the understanding of complexity as a characteristic of systems became established.

By the end of the 1960s, we can see the paradigm of systems in organizations as presented in a collection of articles edited by Fred E. Emery in a volume titled *Systems Thinking* (Emery, 1969). Emery was one of the pioneers in the post–World War II human relations movement, particularly within socio-technical systems theory. In the book, readers are given an overview of some of the basic ideas and key contributors to the rise of systems thinking in the understanding of humans and organizations. Two of those contributors were the Austrian biologist and philosopher Ludwig von Bertalanffy and the Hungarian-born American psychiatrist Andras Angyal, both of whom conducted their doctoral research at the University of Vienna in the 1920s. Bertalanffy was awarded his degree in theoretical biology in 1926, while Angyal was awarded his degree in psychology in 1927. Holism was a topic in both biology and psychology at the time, and both Angyal and Bertalanffy took a strong interest in closely related problems to do with the meaning of holism in living organisms and humans.

The Rise of Systems Thinking in Science:
From Physics to Biology

In 1950, Bertalanffy wrote a seminal article for the journal *Science*, in which he laid out the principles of his theory of open systems in physics and biology for an English-reading audience (Bertalanffy, 1950a). According to his own accounts, he started to work on the open systems theory in 1932. However, in the article he refers also to a publication from 1929 in which he introduced the two principles of his 'organismic theory' (Drack et al., 2007, p. 19).

The organismic theory's *first principle* is that an organized biological system is an *open system* in *flux equilibrium*, meaning that the biological organism maintains itself through a continuous flux of matter and energy in and out of the containment of the organism. It is not in static equilibrium, but in movement, such that it can perform work by keeping itself in a flexible equilibrium while it imports, transforms, and exports energy and matter. The organism has a metabolic property that is essential to its sustainability.

The *second principle* of the organismic theory is that the biological system strives for maximum morphosis, which in German is named *Gestaltheit* (Drack et al., 2007, p. 19). Later, this became the principle of hierarchization, also known as the principle of progressive organization (Bertalanffy, 1932, pp. 269–274, 300–320). The dynamic interactions in the system give rise to order at increasingly higher hierarchical levels. The latter characteristic is the inherent trend towards increasing complexity, a process that Bertalanffy later called *anamorphosis* – a term he had adopted from the German zoologist Richard Woltereck (Drack et al., 2007, p. 19). Besides the principles of dynamics and wholeness, a third one, namely that of primary activity of the organism, became explicit in 1937 (ibid., p. 19).

Bertalanffy's assumption was that, within every living organism, there is a dynamic process. Despite these dynamics, organisms have an intrinsic ability to be drawn towards equilibrium or stability, which he called *dynamic equilibrium*, in contrast to static equilibrium. An organism, whether a cell or a more complex organism, has to perform flexibility in dealing with the exchange of energy and matter in relation to its environment. Furthermore, Bertalanffy proposed that organisms do not fit into a traditional description of a closed system in kinetic reversible equilibrium. They are open to the environment, but still restrained. Hence, they are described as *open systems* (Bertalanffy, 1950a).

From Biology to Psychology

In common with Bertalanffy, Andras Angyal was concerned with the meaning of the idea of wholes. In his pioneering book published in 1941, *Foundations for a Science of Personality* (Angyal, 1941), he claimed this was the most difficult problem for his goal of a science of personality. He noted that the problem was general, which was why he set out to construct some general ideas of wholes that would be useful in his area of interest and beyond. Angyal drew attention to the developments that had been ongoing for decades in biology and psychology:

> In the course of the past two decades it has been almost generally recognized by biologists and psychologists that the clarification of the problem of wholes is essential for progress in the study of the organism. The increasing awareness of the problem of wholes led to the discovery of certain general principles, best formulated perhaps by the Gestalt psychologists.
>
> (Angyal, 1969 [1941], pp. 25–26)

Gestalt psychology is a research direction credited as having been created and developed by Max Wertheimer, Wolfgang Köhler, and Kurt Koffka in Frankfurt, from around 1910 (see Ellis, 1938; Lewin, 1948; Henle, 1961, for collections of important contributions to the research field).

Angyal goes on to explain that the difference between aggregates and systems is that '[i]n aggregates it is significant that the parts are added; in a system it is significant that the parts are arranged' (Angyal, 1969 [1941], p. 26). He also differentiated between wholes and systems: 'I propose that the term whole be reserved to designate the concrete organized object, while the organization itself, the way of arrangements of parts, should be called a system' (ibid., p. 28).

Angyal called for strict logical formulation and compliance with systems principles in order to create what he called a *good system*. This does not allow much for dynamics and must be seen foremost as an expression of an early attempt to define a holistic systems idea that was nevertheless leaning heavily towards logic, mechanical ideas, and closed systems. There is no trace in Angyal's discussion of what complexity means as a result of interactions between units. The new level of order in the case of a whole person seems simply to have been a result of the parts being arranged in an organized way.

As a psychiatrist, Angyal was looking for practical help in a field that lacked both explanations and treatment. However, in common with Bertalanffy, Angyal aimed at a form of fusion between the opposite ideas of reductionism and holism by holding on to the notion that being *scientific* must be based on logic and mathematics. This meant finding a mathematical description for wholes:

> Here the attempt will be made to demonstrate that there is a logical genus suitable to the treatment of wholes. We propose to call it system. . . . The ideal would be to develop a logic of systems to such a degree of precision that it might offer the basis for exact mathematical formulation of holistic connections.
>
> (Angyal, 1969 [1941], p. 17)

The quotation reflects Angyal's hope of finding general rules for holistic systems, much like the hope articulated by Ludwig von Bertalanffy.

From Biology to Ideology

Angyal and Bertalanffy continued to promote their ideas, although in very different ways. After World War II, Bertalanffy immigrated to Canada. By the time he arrived there in 1949, Angyal had already been in the United States for 17 years and was a respected psychiatrist who, among other things, had had his influential book published. Bertalanffy had to start anew, hiding the dark fact that his migration was an escape from the post-war denazification process in Austria, which left him dismissed from his position as professor at the University of Vienna (Pouvreau, 2014, p. 175), a position that had been facilitated by his Nazi Party membership and pledge of allegiance to Hitler already in 1938. He had then eagerly taken up a post with the clear intention of replacing his former teacher, Professor Hans Przibram, who had been dismissed along with all other Jewish scholars (Pouvreau, 2009, p. 67). In 1943, both Przibram and his wife were deported to the concentration camp Theresienstadt, where they perished in 1944, while Bertalanffy continued to link his increasingly omnipotent 'organismic' theory of hierarchical order in all types of organisms, including humans, to fit with Hitler's National Socialism (ibid., p. 63).

However, grand ideas were not new to Bertalanffy. Already in 1934, he had written about how holism, hierarchical, and superior order matched with ideas of the *Führerprinzip* (Bertalanffy, 1934, p. 352, cited in Pouvreau, 2009, p. 65). Even after World War II, while restarting his career in Canada, Bertalanffy maintained contact with the former SS physician Alfred von Auersberg, who had escaped to Chile. Bertalanffy had considered joining Auersberg in Chile in 1950, at the same time as his ideas were becoming known in North America (Pouvreau, 2009, p. 63).

Is Bertalanffy's dark political behaviour significant when we consider the validity of the idea of organizations as holistic systems, which gained dominance in the Western world in the decades after the war? According to David Pouvreau, who during his doctoral research went through all letters and papers in Bertalanffy's remaining archive, which had been discovered in Canada in 2006, 'This background should be borne in mind when considering his first discourses on general systemology' (Pouvreau, 2014, p. 179). Pouvreau also concludes that Bertalanffy's Nazi engagement was a result of his opportunism rather than scientific research:

> All these considerations seem to lead us to the conclusion that Bertalanffy, who entered the NSDAP [National Socialist German Workers' Party, the Nazi Party] of his own free will, did it above all out of opportunism with the hope of giving a powerful impetus to his career and of finally obtaining a position at the university which he had long coveted in vain.
>
> (Pouvreau, 2009, p. 66)

Bertalanffy's opportunism could only have been matched by his lack of ethics, as he seemed at best indifferent to, and at worst eager to please, the terror regime he supported at the expense of his colleagues. Given the fate of his former teacher, there is no reason to assume that Bertalanffy did not know about the persecutions of the Jews. At the height of his support for the Nazi regime, he had an article published in 1941 in *Der Biologie* (English translation: *The Biologist*), which was the official journal of national-socialist biology directly under the supervision of Heinrich Himmler (ibid., p. 73). In the article, Bertalanffy reiterated the unification of his organismic theory with National Socialism (ibid., p. 74), a claim that had nothing whatsoever to do with science. The article was harshly criticized by, among others, the Austrian-British liberal economist and later Nobel Laureate in economic sciences Frederick Hayek. In Bertalanffy's pursuit to become recognized as a great scientist and philosopher in the Third Reich, he constructed a speculative biological theory that would suit the political atmosphere and grant him status at the same time.

Bertalanffy's further career in Canada and the United States is detailed by similar opportunistic behaviour. When systems theory became widely used in the late 1960s, he hurried to claim that he was its pioneer because he had suggested the idea of a general systems theory in 1945 (Bertalanffy, 1968, p. viii). However, as Angyal referred to, those ideas had been around for decades before that. Bertalanffy's version of the theory in the 1930s was set in the context of Nazism, and he had then subsequently reoriented it to fit with whatever would be to his advantage. In 1951, without any reference to Angyal, Bertalanffy suddenly wrote an article on the usefulness of his perspective in psychology (Bertalanffy, 1951b). Pouvreau (2014, p. 179) comments on the article as follows:

> His 1951 paper on theoretical models in psychology is a typical indicator of the concrete effect of this reorientation. Publishing his project was apparently a means for Bertalanffy to optimize his chances to open new academic doors to his career, overcoming his Viennese slump.

General Systems Theory: The Dream of Unifying Science and Society

While open systems theory was an attempt to create a scientific basis for the nature of living organisms, general systems theory was more of an ideology, a programme intended to direct and frame studies in all scientific fields within a common way of thinking. In many ways, the ideology can be seen as an alternative to the human project of science, which thus far had been based on ideas of rational thought, logic, empirical observation, and application of the scientific method. In the 19th century, biology had presented great problems to these ideas in physical science. Science was a programme of reductionism, which was an idea of splitting and isolating reality in ever-smaller parts to find the laws directly governing nature. Biology and open systems theory suggested a different understanding of living entities. If an organism behaves differently from that of the separate parts of which it is built then organisms, animals, human life, and society cannot be understood through the approach of reductionism, classical physical science and mathematics. However, if classical science as a human project was not to be abandoned, how could the science of the inanimate and the realities of life be bridged?

The introduction of general systems theory marked an attempt to solve the problem of bridging physical science (physics) and life science (biology) by arguing for a bold expansion into unexplored territory. It proposed to address problems on *all* scales of reality in the same way, so that researchers in the various sciences could learn from each other through cross-disciplinary collaboration. As the problems facing society and technology did not fall neatly into the categories of traditional knowledge fields, but rather spanned the fields, they were not only in need of collaboration between traditionally separated areas of research but also in need of new fields to be invented in the 'grey zones' between those areas. In order to communicate and coordinate knowledge, some common ground was needed, such as a common language, concepts, principles, and most importantly a common understanding of the ontological basis upon which the general project of all sciences should be set. This was the purpose that it was hoped general systems theory would achieve. It was not so much a theory as an ideology to encompass common ground – an ontological envelope for a view of the world understood as systems.

The idea of opens systems had a long history, but it was only from the mid-1950s onwards that the claim of a general systems theory resonated in different disciplines that supported the idea of developing multidisciplinary approaches. When Bertalanffy promoted general systems theory as a new paradigm for the model construction of all sciences (Bertalanffy, 1950b, 1951a), it was portrayed as a qualitative theory, the purpose of which was to implicate universal principles to guide all systems, or rather all knowledge *as* systems (Caws, 2015). Organisms, human organizations, and societies were to be seen as if they were open systems with interrelated subsystems that were mutually dependent on each other. Open systems were seen as coupled together with the environment of which they also were a part. Conceptually, such a system is a complex unit in space and time with structural similarities (i.e. isomorphisms). Systemic parts sustain the structure through a structuring process, which tends to restore itself after disturbances, analogous to properties of a living organism. As these isomorphisms were seen to exist in the same structural form, whether they were living organisms, organizations, society, or even as 'thinking' machines, the idea emerged that one could simulate models and transfer data from one scientific discipline to another, and from the models to the real world (Bertalanffy, 1968; Van Gigch, 1974).

Researchers in a range of knowledge fields were welcoming unifying ideas in the post-war Western world. Social theory before World War II was very much divided between those who believed that the social sciences should be based on the physical sciences and those who believed in its foundation in a social theory of human interaction linked to the ideas in *philosophical pragmatism* (Blumer, 1937; Joas and Knöbl, 2009). Pragmatism as a philosophical direction argued for the importance of human experience, social interaction, and creativity as the basis for understanding the human condition.

Leading pragmatists such as John Dewey regarded science as a very important human endeavour to engage in, but not as a project to form general external laws that would explain, determine, and rule humanity and society itself (Dewey, 1910).

The idea of a general systems theory did not endure within physics and chemistry, and eventually it dwindled within biology too, perhaps because the ideas were too much in conflict with the scientific method. At a time where there was a strong belief in the progress of natural science and technology, general systems theory implied a view in opposition to traditional scientific thinking. It was an ambitious ideology to colonize all sciences at the expense of classical science.

However, the place where the idea stuck was in the social sciences, a field that had been weakened by the pre-war disputes about its philosophical foundation. There, systems theory resonated with the work of Parsons (1937) and his structuralist social theory. Parsons completely discarded the views of pragmatism, and as his theory became the dominant and unifying social theory in the 1950s and 1960s, pragmatism became marginalized (Joas and Knöbl, 2009). Later, the influential German sociologist Niklas Luhmann, in his book *Social Systems* (Luhmann, 1995), originally published in German in 1984, boosted further interest in a purified version of a general systems theory in social theory (Joas and Knöbl, 2009).

Parsonian structuralism influenced a post-war generation of organization theorists, among them James March and Herbert Simon, who contributed by framing organizational studies as part of what came to be known in the United States from the 1950s as *behavioural sciences* (March and Simon, 1993). Nevertheless, Bertalanffy's background and dreams of a general systems ideology – a systemology for all sciences – show that the systems ideology did not rest on any real scientific process. The framing and even imprisonment of organizational theory within a dominant systems ideology is a very important point to note because it meant that complexity as a theme in organizations also became framed within the same ideology.

References

Angyal, A. (1941). *Foundations for a Science of Personality*. Cambridge, MA: Harvard University Press.

Angyal, A. (1969 [1941]). A logic of systems. In: Emery, F.E. (ed.) *Systems Thinking: Selected Readings*, pp. 17–29. Hammondsworth, UK: Penguin Books.

Bertalanffy, L. von (1932). *Theoretiche Biologie – I. Band: allgemenine Theorie, Physikochemie, Aufbau und Entwicklung des Organismus*. Berlin: Gebrüder Borntraeger, pp. 269–274, 300–320.

Bertalanffy, L. von (1934). Wandlungen des biologischen Denkens. *Neue Jahrbücher für Wissenschaft und Jugendbildung* 10, pp. 339–366.

Bertalanffy, L. von (1950a). The theory of open systems in physics and biology. *Science New Series* 111(2872), pp. 23–29. American Association for the Advancement of Science.

Bertalanffy, L. von (1950b). An outline of a general system theory. *British Journal of Philosophy of Science* 1, pp. 134–165.

Bertalanffy, L. von (1951a). General systems theory: A new approach to unity of science. *Human Biology* 23, pp. 303–361.

Bertalanffy, L. von (1951b). Theoretical models in biology and psychology. *Journal of Personality* 20, pp. 24–38.

Bertalanffy, L. von (1968). *General Systems Theory*. New York: George Braziller.

Blumer, H. (1937). Social psychology. In: Schmidt, E.P. (ed.) *Man and Society*, pp. 144–198. New York: Prentice-Hall.

Boulding, K. (1956). General systems theory: The skeleton of science. *Management Science* 2(3), pp. 197–208.

Bruce, K. (2006). Henry S. Dennison, Elton Mayo, and human relations historiography. *Management & Organizational History* 1(2), pp. 177–199.

Caws, P. (2015). General systems theory: Its past and potential. *Systems Research and Behavioral Science* 32(5), pp. 514–521.

Copeland, B.J. (2004). *The Essential Turing: Seminal Writings in Computing, Logic, Philosophy, Artificial Intelligence, and Artificial Life Plus the Secrets of the Enigma*. Oxford: Oxford University Press.

Dewey, J. (1910). Science as subject-matter and as method. *Science New Series* 31(787), pp. 121–127. American Association for the Advancement of Science.

Drack, M., Apfalter, W. & Pouvreau, D. (2007). On the making of a system theory of life: Paul A. Weiss and Ludwig von Bertalanffy's conceptual connection. *Quarterly Review of Biology* 82(4), pp. 349–373.

Ellis, W.D. (ed.) (1938). *A Source Book of Gestalt Psychology*. London: Routledge.

Emery, F.E. (ed.) (1969). *Systems Thinking*. Hammondsworth: Penguin Books.

Emery, F.E. & Trist, E.L. (1960). *Socio-Technical Systems in Management Science: Models and Techniques*. Oxford: Pergamon Press.

Follett, M.P. (1923). *The New State: Group Organization and the Solution of Popular Government*. New York: Longmans, Green and Co.

Follett, M.P. (1926). The psychological foundations of business administration. In: Metcalf, H.C. (ed.) *The Scientific Foundations of Business Administration*, pp. 30–69. Baltimore, MD: The Williams and Wilkins Company.

Forrester, J.W. (1961). *Industrial Dynamics*. Cambridge, MA: Productivity Press.

Henle, M. (ed.) (1961). *Documents of Gestalt Psychology*. Los Angeles, CA: University of California Press.

16   *Foundations of Complexity*

Joas, H. & Knöbl, W. (2009). *Social Theory: Twenty Introductory Lectures*. Cambridge: Cambridge University Press.

Katz, D. & Kahn, R.L. (1966). *The Social Psychology of Organizations*. New York: John Wiley.

Lewin, K. (1948). *Resolving Social Conflicts: Selected Papers on Group Dynamics*. New York: Harper & Row.

Likert, R. (1947). Kurt Lewin: A pioneer in human relations research. *Human Relations* 1(1), pp. 131–140.

Luhmann, N. (1995). *Social Systems*. Stanford, CA: Stanford University Press.

March, J.G. & Simon, H.A. (1993). *Organizations*. 2nd ed. Cambridge, MA: Blackwell.

Mayo, E. (1933). *The Human Problems of an Industrial Civilization*. New York: Viking Press.

Mayo, E. (1949). *The Social Problems of Industrial Civilization*. London: Routledge.

Parsons, T. (1937). *The Structure of Social Action*. New York: McGraw-Hill.

Pouvreau, D. (2009). *The Dialectical Tragedy of the Concept of Wholeness: Ludwig von Bertalanffy's Biography Revisited*. Litchfield Park, AZ: ISCE.

Pouvreau, D. (2014). On the history of Ludwig von Bertalanffy's 'general systemology', and on its relationship to cybernetics – Part II: Contexts and developments of the systemological hermeneutics instigated by von Bertalanffy. *International Journal of General Systems* 43(2), pp. 172–245.

Roethlisberger, F.J. & Dickson, W.J. (1939). *Management and the Worker*. Cambridge, MA: Harvard University Press.

Taylor, F. (1911). *Principles of Scientific Management*. New York: Harper & Bros.

Trist, E. & Bamforth, K.W. (1951). Some social and psychological consequences of the long wall method of coal getting. *Human Relations* 4, pp. 3–38.

Van Gigch, J.P. (1974). *Applied General Systems Theory*. New York: Harper & Row.

Weaver, W. (1948). Science and complexity. *American Scientist* 36(4), pp. 536–544.

Wiener, N. (1948). *Cybernetics: Or Control and Communication in the Animal and the Machine*. 1st ed. Cambridge: MA: MIT Press.

2 Cybernetics

The Rise of a Systems Science to Control Complexity

Computers, Biology, and Society

Just after World War II, around the same time as Ludwig von Bertalanffy left the ashes of Austria and started to promote his idea in the English-speaking world of a general systems approach to science, the American mathematician Norbert Wiener, who was from a very different place and background, had a book published that was eventually to become very influential in 'systems science' (Wiener, 1948). Wiener introduced the term cybernetics to a world where researchers and industrial and military leaders were looking enthusiastically for new ideas in the landscape between technology, the natural sciences, and the social sciences. The term cybernetics had been mentioned earlier in history, in 1834 by the physicist André Ampère, who described it as the art of governing nations (Keller, 2008, p. 64), but the term had not been used to bridge engineering, biology, and the social sciences until World War II had prompted innovations that stimulated ideas of a closer integration between man and machine.

The first electronic computer, ENIAC, had been designed during the war and was put into practical use in February 1946. Its much improved follower – the Electronic Discrete Variable Automatic Computer (EDVAC) – had already been proposed by the inventors of ENIAC, John Mauchly and J. Presper Eckert. They received help from the brilliant and highly influential mathematician and computer pioneer John von Neumann, who in 1945 had drafted a report on the EDVAC's functionality and logic design (Neumann, 1993 [1945]). The computer was eventually built and started its operation from 1951. Neumann, a professor of mathematics at Princeton University at the age of 29 years, and by many considered the foremost mathematician of his time, was also a pioneer of game theory (Neumann and Morgenstern, 1944) and a key strategic and scientific figure in the United States' atomic bomb programmes, from the initial Manhattan Project to the construction of the thermonuclear hydrogen

DOI: 10.4324/9781003042501-3

bomb, in the 1950s. Among other things he advised the US government and promoted the central nuclear arms race doctrine of Mutual Assured Destruction, a game theory idea that was made real by the development of small nuclear warheads that could fit onto intercontinental rockets and guarantee nuclear retaliation anywhere in the world.

In contrast to Neumann, Norbert Wiener refused to take funding from military projects and instead warned against the militarization of science (Wiener, 1947, 1985 [1947]). Wiener, who was a professor of mathematics at Massachusetts Institute of Technology (MIT) and a pioneer in computer science and automation, wanted to use technology to improve people's lives, especially in poor countries. His ideas of humanity, ethics, and the purpose of science, including critical views on nuclear weapons, stood in sharp contrast to Neumann's eagerly provided assistance to military atomic bomb programmes (Heims, 1980).

Nevertheless, both Neumann and Wiener, as well as many other important figures in mathematics, engineering, psychology, and the social sciences at the time, met and exchanged ideas in the context of the special series of Macy conferences, which started in New York in 1946 with the conference title 'Feedback Mechanisms and Circular Causal Systems in Biological and Social Systems'. The conference series continued with cybernetics as the main theme, until 1953, and was subsequently followed by a series of conferences on group processes from 1954 to 1960 (Heims, 1991). Chaired by the neurophysiologist and psychiatry professor Warren S. McCulloch, the Macy conferences pioneered cross-disciplinary and multidisciplinary approaches by bringing researchers from different disciplines together to discuss complex problems outside the formal channels of publication. It was an important breeding ground for the new field of cybernetics, which was a term included in the conference programme in 1948 after the publication of Wiener's book. The conferences included emerging research fields that explored the relation between the brain, mind, and behaviour, such as neuroscience and cognitive psychology. Moreover, the conference discussions included the fields of organization, management, as well as general political and social issues.

Heims (1991) argues that, in addition to Norbert Wiener, John von Neumann, and Warren S. McCulloch, the most important figure in the rise of cybernetics was the British anthropologist Gregory Bateson, who was one of the members of the core group of contributors throughout the Macy conference series on cybernetics and group processes from 1946 to 1960. He was also part of the early interdisciplinary discussions in conferences preceding the Macy conferences and later influenced cross-disciplinary, cultural, and organizational studies, particularly after the first edition of his book *Steps to an Ecology of Mind* was published (Bateson, 1972).

At the first Macy conference in March 1946, Bateson presented his theory of learning as a challenge for machines, distinguishing between learning and learning how to learn. It is noteworthy that much later the organizational theorists Chris Argyris and Donald Schön adopted the exact same distinction as proposed by Bateson in their theory of organizational learning. Their concepts for the same ideas were called single-loop learning and double-loop learning, clearly using the language of cybernetic feedback loops to understand human learning and psychology (Argyris and Schön, 1978, 1996). Thereby, Argyris and Schön placed themselves within the branch of cognitive psychology, and thus represent another example of the strong links that were established between organizational theory, the American behavioural science movement, and the cybernetic branch of the systems science movement.

In cognitive psychological theory, cybernetic ideas of technological process control were taken up and morphed into a theory of feedback and error correction. The human brain was seen as resembling a computer (Gardner, 1985). In recent decades, cognitive psychology has further expanded into various forms of behavioural therapy dealing with a wide spectrum of psychological and mental problems. This modern diffusion of applications of ideas from technological systems control to the core processes of human identity and existence strongly echoes Andras Angyal's hope in the early 1940s for systems theory as a way to understand human personality and its disorders (see Chapter 1). Despite its claim of being based on science, cognitive behavioural therapy has been criticized recently for being more political and speculative than scientifically sound (Dalal, 2018). It is clear that the politics of the rise of a systems science and of complexity as a theme in organizations have been immersed in a paradoxical struggle between, on the one hand, a wish to bridge the natural sciences and the human sciences, and, on the other hand, an ambition that this fusion should be based on some reliable and valid foundation that could generally be termed *scientific*, even though it has been far from clear what a general science would look like.

Neumann and Wiener both argued that their cybernetic theories would be useful in economics and political science. In order to attract social scientists to hear and discuss new ideas, the Macy foundation had Bateson arrange a subconference in 1946, titled 'Teleological Mechanisms in Society' (Heims, 1991). Two of the most influential post-war thinkers in American social theory, Talcott Parsons and Robert Merton, attended the subconference, during which Kurt Lewin (the German-American social psychologist who had pioneered research into human relations and group dynamics) gave a presentation on concepts of Gestalt psychology, after which it was recommended that the concepts should be discussed further at later conferences.

Another of the pioneers of Gestalt psychology, Wolfgang Köhler, was invited to speak at the third in the series of special Macy conferences, although there were concerns among some participants about the focus on Köhler's thinking. A rift was opening between what was seen as the soft approach of Gestalt psychology and the hard approach of mathematics, neurophysiology, and cybernetics. By the tenth Macy conference in 1953, it was evident that the technological approach of cybernetics and the biological approach of Gestalt psychology had drifted so far apart that the conference series on cybernetics, biology, and society ended (Heims, 1991).

Wiener's cybernetics was a science of communication control through feedback loops and alluded to a homology between animals and machines (Keller, 2008, p. 65). According to this theory, any system, living or not, must have some form of negative feedback mechanism. Wiener compared the regulation of organisms to thermostats. Referring to Cannon (1932) and his idea of homeostasis, which was based on the work of the 19th-century French physiologist Claude Bernard, Wiener repeated the theory that the human body depends on homeostatic processes, that life in equilibrium is active and dynamic, and that 'each deviation from the norm brings on a reaction in the opposite direction, which is of the nature of what we call negative feedback' (Wiener, 1948, p. 251).

On the other side of the Atlantic, the British psychiatrist William Ross Ashby was an early contributor to the rise of cybernetics. His article on self-organizing machines was published in the late 1940s (Ashby, 1947). Ashby's primary concern was with the nervous system, particularly its ability to regulate and reorganize, with resulting changed behaviour (Keller, 2008, p. 67). In an article published in 1948, he reported that he had built a machine that could fulfil the dual criteria of both being determinate in its action (referring to its mechanical limits and form), and at the same time induce in itself a change of organization (and thus resemble biological self-organization). This, he thought, could serve as a primitive model of a living brain (ibid., p. 67). He called the machine a *homeostat* (Ashby, 1948, p. 380).

Ashby's thinking about the human nervous system as a machine, which for him was directly linked to human behaviour, even took the form of arguing that homeostatic regulation (negative feedback) was tantamount to being ethical. If what he called a human system was self-organizing, it would mean that a change was automatically made to the feedback in order to regulate it from positive feedback (i.e. not in control) to negative feedback (i.e. in control). Ashby argued that the basis for such mechanisms (positive and negative) in the human brain would be a change from bad to good organization (i.e. behaviour).

In March 1952, Ashby linked up with the American mathematicians and cyberneticists as a guest at the ninth Macy conference, during which he presented two papers, one on the homeostat and one on chess-playing machines. The conference that was supposed to bring different disciplines together was at that time already dissolving into sub-disciplines. Conflicts had to do not only with the personalities of the people involved (Gefter, 2015) but also with fundamentally different views on human beings between those who took a technical mathematical approach to learning and humans and those who argued that such approaches had serious limitations.

Thinking Machines

In the late 1940s and throughout the 1950s, various attempts were made towards the creation of thinking machines. Keller (2008, p. 69) refers to the story of Frank Rosenblatt, who, inspired by the work of Hebb (1949) and Neumann (1958) on self-reproducing automata, and financially aided by the military and Cornell University, attempted to build a 'perceptron', a machine that would be able to perform its own perceptions and identifications of the environment without human training. The machine was intented to be able to reproduce and to have a form of awareness of its own existence.

The interest in cybernetics on the part of the military was clear: they wanted a machine that could learn and behave autonomously. In pursue of such a machine, conferences on what the military termed *self-organization* were arranged throughout the 1960s (Keller, 2008, p. 70). However, for Ashby and others, the term self-organizing did not make any sense for an isolated machine; it only made sense if a machine were coupled to another machine. Ashby took a connectionist view of self-organization, a point that we would do well to note today. The emergence of the Internet has strengthened the idea that endless connections between machines can produce results that no one can control. In this sense, Ashby's dream of self-organizing machines has been more than fulfilled. In many ways, so too has Rosenblatt's dream if we think about how communication technologies are integrated into our lives and behaviour, and how research continues to integrate nanotechnologies, genetic engineering, and biotechnological techniques into animals and humans.

However, by the end of the 1960s, cybernetics had collapsed as a direction within developmental biology and engineering (Keller, 2008, p. 72). Funding from the military dried up in favour of the emergent field of *artificial intelligence*. The 'perceptron' was never built; moreover, no other machine that could live up to Wiener's homology between machine and organisms was built (ibid., p. 74). However, cybernetics was not dead in organizational and management studies – quite the opposite.

Norbert Wiener's speculative ideas and wishful thinking ended up being adopted by a generation of organizational and management scientists and consultants who were looking for some kind of legitimization and basis in a field that lacked it. Ludwig von Bertalanffy's ideas of open systems and of a general systems theory (see Chapter 1) became established within the field of organizational studies in concert with the rise of a 'systems science' from the 1950s onwards. The ideas, which assumed that organizations are open systems in need of regulation by cybernetic principles in order to stabilize in equilibrium, were consistently and explicitly articulated by pioneering thinkers in organizational theory.

In the first issue of the journal *Human Relations*, Kurt Lewin wrote about group dynamics in relation to social equilibrium (Lewin, 1947). One decade later, March and Simon (1958), in their seminal text on organizations, invoked the brainchild of cybernetics – cognitive psychology – to examine human behaviour in organizations, assuming that equilibrium was the best condition for an organization's survival. The idea that organizations and even national states ought to be regulated to equilibrium in order to control complexity is to this day widespread in politics, social science, organizational studies, and management theory.

Taylorism 2.0: Cybernetic Control of Complexity in Organizations

The integration of cybernetics in systems theories meant a comeback of Taylorism (Shafritz and Ott, 2001, p. 242). Systems theories typically made use of quantitative tools to understand complex relationships and to optimize decisions, and the theories became the basis of quasi-scientific fields such as management sciences and administrative sciences. As such, they were just a semantic distance from Taylor's theory of scientific management (ibid., p. 243). The fusion of open systems and cybernetics resonated with Bertalanffy's idea of a global programme for all sciences – a general systems theory or, more precisely translated from German, *a general systemology*.

However, Bertalanffy argued that there is a fundamental difference between a general systems theory and cybernetics, since the mechanisms for feedback in cybernetics are controlled by limitations, while in dynamic systems there is a free flow of forces and energy. Furthermore, in machines, cybernetic self-regulating mechanisms are based on predetermined structures. This indicates a need to study the dynamic properties of systems. Bertalanffy claimed that general systems theory included cybernetic theory as a special class of self-regulating systems (Bertalanffy, 1968, p. 17). By contrast, Bertalanffy's theory of open systems was built on the assumption that hierarchical organization in nature and society are in dynamic equilibrium. However, the only way to keep an organization intentionally in equilibrium was thought to be by establishing external regulating loops or cybernetic control systems. These two opposing ideas, that organizations are open and dynamic yet need to be regulated and controlled by negative feedback systems (in the form of management control systems), became the two most fundamental principles of modern management theory and organizational theory.

The Cybernetic Society

Nowhere was the link between cybernetics and management practice more clearly promoted than in the case of the British business consultant and professor Stafford Beer, whose work ranged from experimenting with computer-aided operational management in the British company United Steel in the 1950s to aiding various governments on centralized economic decision-making systems, among them the Chilean socialist president Salvador Allende's government. Beer wrote a number of books with titles clearly reflecting his way of thinking about management, such as *Management and Cybernetics* (Beer, 1959), *Decision and Control* (Beer, 1966), *Management Science* (Beer, 1968), and *Brain of the Firm* (Beer, 1972).

The idea behind Beer's books was the desire to gain full control by entering all information into computers that could process and aid in correcting any deviation from the decided course. It was Taylorism returning in a new 'fancy dress', and this time managers did not have to bother about inspecting the shop floor in order to be in control; they could sit and assess the data on their screens in operations rooms, where all information needed for decision-making streamed in and out. When applied to the administration of society, the new version of Taylorism was as if it had taken inspiration from George Orwell's novel *1984*, in which Big Brother – the State – is watching everyone and everything (Orwell, 1949). For state governments with an appetite for centralized control, the possibility of applying computer tools for surveillance of society must have sounded as a dream come true. However, in Chile, before the grand system of control could be installed and operated, a United States-led military coup was tearing down the government – installing chaos and terror instead of control. Beer himself, a creative, independent soul and flamboyant character, who clearly favoured his own freedom, retreated to a small cottage in Wales, as far away as possible from any intrusive control regimes.

To this day, every instrumental management idea that has been implemented through computerized control systems, performance systems, and various feedback systems in organizations is born from a belief in the principles of cybernetics to regulate human behaviour in organizations. In many, if not most textbooks used in business schools and universities that educate leaders, we can find the view that organizations are systems that are best regulated and controlled by cybernetic feedback mechanisms installed and operated by bureaucrats and managers. This way of thinking has expanded to become the mainstream in the management of business as well as public organizations. The reasoning is as follows.

In order to be in control, managers in organizations should install control mechanisms. From an imagined detached position relative to – or outside of – the organization, the managers are believed to overview the whole of the larger system (environment) in which the organization is a part. The managers should then be able to hold the organization and its trajectory under strategic and operational control while moving towards a future that is uncertain yet controllable as long as signals from the outside and the inside of the organization reach the management and their computerized feedback systems early enough for them to react. Based on the information received, they react by making decisions, which they then feed back into the organization, and in that way adjust the organization (as a whole) to the environment so that it keeps itself in a dynamic equilibrium, and so moves in a controlled way towards the future or, more precisely, through time and space. The idea is that any experience of complexity (e.g. unpredictability) is kept under control in this way.

References

Argyris, C. & Schön, D. (1978). *Organizational Learning: A Theory of Action Perspective*. Reading, MA: Addison-Wesley.

Argyris, C. & Schön, D. (1996). *Organizational Learning II: Theory, Method and Practice*. Reading, MA: Addison-Wesley.

Ashby, W.R. (1947). Principles of the self-organizing dynamic system. *Journal of General Psychology* 37, pp. 125–128.

Ashby, W.R. (1948). The homeostat. *Electron* 20, p. 380.

Bateson, G. (1972). *Steps to an Ecology of Mind: Collected Essays in Anthropology, Psychiatry, Evolution, and Epistemology*. Chicago, IL: University of Chicago Press.

Beer, S. (1959). *Cybernetics and Management*. London: English Universities Press.

Beer, S. (1966). *Decision and Control*. London: Wiley.

Beer, S. (1968). *Management Science*. London: Aldus Books.

Beer, S. (1972). *Brain of the Firm*. London: Penguin Press.

Bertalanffy, L. von (1968). *General Systems Theory*. New York: George Braziller.

Cannon, W.B. (1932). *The Wisdom of the Body*. New York: W.W. Norton.

Dalal, F. (2018). *The Cognitive Behavioural Tsunami: Managerialism, Politics and the Corruptions of Science*. London: Routledge.

Gardner, H. (1985). *The Mind's New Science: A History of the Cognitive Revolution*. New York: Basic Books.

Gefter, A. (2015). The man who tried to redeem the world with logic. *Nautilus* 5 February, p. 21: Information. nautil.us/issue/21/information (accessed 5 July 2021).

Hebb, D.O. (1949). *The Organization of Behaviour*. New York: Wiley.

Heims, S.J. (1980). *John von Neumann and Norbert Wiener: From Mathematics to the Technologies*. Cambridge, MA: MIT Press.

Heims, S.J. (1991). *The Cybernetics Group*. Cambridge, MA: MIT Press.

Keller, E.F. (2008). Organisms, machines, and thunderstorms: A history of self-organization, part one. *Historical Studies in the Natural Sciences* 38(1), pp. 45–75.

Lewin, K. (1947). Frontiers in group dynamics: Concept, method and reality in social science: Social equilibrium and social change. *Human Relations* 1(1), pp. 5–41.

March, J.G. & Simon, H.A. (1958). *Organizations*. 1st ed. New York: John Wiley & Sons.

Neumann, J. von (1958). *The Computer and the Brain*. New Haven, CT: Yale University Press.

Neumann, J. von (1993 [1945]). First draft of a report on the EDVAC. *IEEE Annals of the History of Computing* 15(4), pp. 27–43.

Neumann, J. von & Morgenstern, O. (1944). *Theories of Games and Economic Behaviour*. Princeton, NJ: Princeton University Press.

Orwell, G. (1949). *Nineteen Eighty-Four*. London: Secker & Warburg.

Shafritz, J.M. & Ott, J.S. (2001). *Classics of Organization Theory*. 5th ed. Belmont, CA: Wadsworth.

Wiener, N. (1947). The armed services are not fit almoners for education and science. *Bulletin of the Atomic Scientists* 3(8), p. 228.

Wiener, N. (1948). *Cybernetics: Or Control and Communication in the Animal and the Machine*. 1st ed. Cambridge, MA: MIT Press.

Wiener, N. (1985 [1947]). A scientist rebels. In: Masani, P. (ed.) *Norbert Wiener, Collected Works with Commentaries*. Volume 4, p. 748. Cambridge, MA: MIT Press.

3 Systems Theories and Complexity in Organizations

Why Did Systems Thinking Rise to Dominance in Organizations?

Systems thinking emerged from a century-long philosophical and scientific discussion about biology's relation to physics, starting with the German philosopher Immanuel Kant, who in his *Critique of Judgement*, published in 1790, addressed the question: What is an organism? (Keller, 2008, pp. 47–48) The discussion concerned how to arrive at a coherent and fundamental scientific theory of life. Furthermore, there was a similarly long-term debate about whether it would be possible to construct a machine that could reproduce itself. If the mechanical laws of nature determined human activity, then surely it was possible to construct a machine that was human? It was not straightforward that out of this discussion a common theory – systems theory – would be taken as the basis for human production, organization, management, and society, and, moreover, that this theory would dominate those areas for decades in post–World War II societies until today. Nevertheless, it did and it has.

One possible reason why systems theory came to dominate in organizational studies was the names and authority of the researchers who supported it. As continental Europe, in general, and Germany, in particular, lay in ruins after the war, the centres of gravity for progress in science and technology moved westwards to the United States and eastwards to the Soviet Union. Already in the 1920s and 1930s there had been a significant movement of talented and brilliant scholars and researchers from Europe to the United States, and this continued after the war. Many of the great names in post-war organizational theory came from a few elite universities in the United States. New research centres were set up, often in financial collaboration with the military or big industry.

It seems clear that the idea of organizations as systems was embraced and promoted by a relatively small network of researchers in the United

DOI: 10.4324/9781003042501-4

States who influenced the field of organizational studies. Those who took interest and promoted the systems idea included influential psychologist James G. Miller at the University of Chicago and later University of Michigan, who in 1949 had coined the expression *behavioural science* to the study of humans and society. He spearheaded the establishment of a *Center for Advanced Study in the Behavioral Sciences* at Stanford University financed by the Ford Foundation (Pouvreau, 2009, pp. 128–130). The centre invited 38 experts to promote interdisciplinary research in the behavioural sciences, among them Bertalanffy and Kenneth Boulding, who taught a seminar where, among others, Herbert Simon participated (ibid., p. 138). Simon, an organizational theorist and later Nobel laureate in economic sciences, was a highly respected professor and administrator at the Carnegie Institute of Technology (later Carnegie-Mellon University). He had also been involved in the administration of the Marshall Aid to Europe after World War II, and later served on President Lyndon B. Johnson's Science Advisory Committee, and at the National Academy of Science. Johnson's secretary of defence, Robert McNamara, came from the Ford Motor Company and was an eager promoter of systems analysis in management and in public administration during the escalation of the Vietnam War. Clearly, the people who in the 1950s met in various contexts to discuss the emerging behavioural sciences and systems thinking strongly influenced the spread of these ideas in the studies and management of organizations.

In the decades to come, systems theory became the state-of-the-art way of thinking about organizations and complexity among researchers around the world. Everyone looked to the centre of scientific, technological, and industrial development – the United States – and consequently the field of organization and management became defined by one single general idea as fixed as any natural law: organizations are systems. However, this idea had no basis in science; it was rather an ideological construct thought to be of practical help.

The argument that academic elites are important for spreading and solidifying ideas and theories is supported by Heims (1991) in his investigations into the rise and spread of cybernetics in the social sciences. His theory stands in contrast to widespread views holding that scientific ideas evolve 'stone by stone' in neutral communities of scientists who are contributing on an equal basis to a knowledge field solely on the merits of quality and validity of their research findings. In the case of systems thinking and its view on complexity, it seems that it penetrated into organizational studies as a result of its promotion by an academic elite in conjunction with the emerging patterns of power in a political-military elite in the interlude between a global destructive war and a global strategic cold war.

Another possible reason for the emergence of the dominance of systems thinking and its associated understanding of complexity in organizational studies is that systems theory offered both a fusion of and a new alternative to two previous conflicting views, both of which in their original form had become criticized in the post-war period. On the one hand, Taylorism and its mechanical view of human work did not match the new world, where democratic structures such as the welfare state, workers' rights, and union participation in work organizations spread in many Western countries. On the other hand, when the human relations movement, at least the Euro-Australian version, evolved into a political movement that focused on democratization of the workplace, and union involvement in organizations (Emery and Thorsrud, 1969), it stretched the tie towards a potential threat to capital ownership. Such approaches were unlikely to have a breakthrough among industry leaders in the United States. Moreover, human relations research focused on the physical working environment and social relations among workers, perspectives that would attract less interest in business schools that were educating leaders to manage primarily the investments and business interests of big companies (corporates).

During the 1950s, the world was becoming more complex, in every sense of the word: engineers had to handle more advanced, dangerous, and dynamic technologies, economists had to deal with dynamic markets, and leaders had to face dynamic international trade and industries. Mass education of skilled knowledge workers was needed in new types of technological industries where gigantic projects ingrained in national security interests fused industrial, military, and societal purposes to the degree that the former five-star general, President Eisenhower, in his farewell address, warned against what he called the 'military-industrial complex' and 'the potential for the disastrous rise of misplaced power' (Eisenhower, 1961).

The 1950s and 1960s was an age of renewal and innovation. There was an eagerness and impatience in the West towards getting ahead of the Soviets in particular. An estimated 2 million Americans contributed to NASA's first human spaceflight programme, Project Mercury, which ran from 1958 to 1963 (National Geographic, n.d.). At its peak, the Apollo programme in the 1960s employed 400,000 people and required the support of over 20,000 industrial firms and universities (NASA, 2008). The technological and human challenges of those companies and their employees were far from those of the British coal mine workers that Trist and Bamforth (1951) studied in the early post-war years from the perspective of human relations theory. Organizational problems associated with a low-skilled workforce in industrial production that involved processing raw materials did not match the new context of high-skilled competitive and innovative industry driven by an ideology-centred political pragmatism.

Organizational theory in the 1950s and 1960s, particularly seen from the American perspective, was in desperate need of renewal. Systems theory offered a solution to the field, namely the inclusion of more or less everything in analyses. In turn, that meant a fusion of hard technological science and computers with human issues. However, to accomplish the fusion, two initially emerging directions would have to be fused: an open systems theory inspired by the science of living organisms (i.e. biology) and cybernetics as the science of machine control (i.e. engineering).

The two ideas would become forged in the strong alliances that were based on general frameworks adopted in terms such as *systems science* and *general systems theory*. The idea of the organization as some sort of system became axiomatic and undisputable. Understanding complexity in organizations became synonymous with understanding complexity in systems (Van Gigch, 1974). However, an organizational complexity theory had not yet been developed.

Systems Dynamics: Expanding the Boundaries and Closing the Systems

In 1956, American industrial engineer Jay Forrester pioneered the field of systems dynamics – a different strain of systems theory than open systems theory and cybernetics. The first full account of the principles and the applications were given in his book *Industrial Dynamics* (Forrester, 1961). During the 1960s, Forrester's approach attracted the attention of industrial leaders, who experienced increasing problems with prediction and stability in industrial production and supply chains. Forrester moved on to critique the simplicity and limitations of traditional planning and policy decision-making processes, and he argued in his book *Urban Dynamics* for the application of systems dynamics computer modelling in ever-larger social and political domains, including urban planning (Forrester, 1969), and eventually the whole planet, in his book *World Dynamics* (Forrester, 1971). Systems dynamics theory promoted a strong belief in what technology and computers could do to help decision makers.

Forrester, in contrast to Bertalanffy, criticized the adoption of models from biology and the physical sciences, and argued that engineering models was closer to social reality with respect to complexity:

> Models in engineering and military usage provide a much better precedent for the social sciences than do physical science and biology models. Economics and management, like engineering, deal with aggregate systems above the level of individual elementary event that are the subject of many physical science models. Unlike systems that

are commonly modelled in the physical sciences, engineering systems have complexity approaching the complexity of social systems.

(Forrester, 1961, p. 53)

Whereas cybernetic control depends on *negative* feedback loops, which feed information back to the source, producing input in such a way that the source dampens or increases the input in accordance with the set target, systems dynamics is concerned with how *positive* feedback loops can cause an organization to spiral out of control until it breaks down. Positive feedback loops are those that feed energy into the source in such a way that the effects increase non-linearly. Systems dynamics theory points to a conglomerate of options for complex systems to have feedback loops integrated into their activity and that, when triggered, could destroy the system very rapidly. Accordingly, it is impossible to control every positive feedback loop, which implies that organizations seen as complex systems will always carry an intrinsic risk of breaking down.

The normal risk of breakdown due to intrinsic positive feedback loops in organizations dealing with complex technologies is what Perrow (1984) alluded to when he used the term 'normal accidents'. He argued that *interactive complexity* and tight coupling of system characteristics inevitably cause such accidents. Perrow treated complexity as an internal uncontrollable property of an otherwise controllable system. The notion of the inevitability of breakdown from complex interdependencies stands in contrast to open systems theory and cybernetics. Open systems theory holds that an organism (and an organization) is capable of adapting to virtually any situation. It has the strength and capacity gained from evolutionary properties to withstand changes in the environment. Moreover, when it comes to disturbances within the organism and/or organization, the negative feedback mechanisms evolve either in concert with or in reaction to the disturbances and therefore contribute to the adaptation process. Perrow's thinking is in line with Forrester's systems dynamics theory and its confinement of analysis to the imagined inside of systems boundaries, which must be defined; hence in Forrester's theory systems are not open and do not resemble physical systems:

> Social systems are strongly characterized by their closed-loop (information-feedback) structure, like many engineering systems that have been modelled but unlike most models in the basic physical sciences.
>
> (Forrester, 1961, p. 53)

It is clear that Forrester's purpose for systems dynamics analysis was to provide decision support for top management or government leaders. Systems analysis should result in decisions directed precisely to where they are effective in order to influence the feedback loops that are in operation within the system model (i.e. the organization). Furthermore, according to Forrester, the objective of systems dynamics analysis was to create *equilibrium* in the system at hand. Forrester saw the ailments of companies and societies as expressions of a system that was distorted and not in a state of equilibrium, or as having pockets of disequilibrium that were greatly influencing the rest of the structure. He referred to systems as *complex*, but he did not present any theory of what complexity is, or any explanation of why it is that people keep making decisions that lead organizations into disequilibrium. Although Forrester identified many of the problems facing social and organizational activity, he failed to realize that the challenges of human and social complexity is more than just a lack of an overview or control that can be helped with computer calculations. What was missing in Forrester's perspective was contact with social theories of organization and what complexity means in human terms, as well as how dynamic phenomena and novelty emerge in organizations.

Institutional and Cultural Perspectives on Complexity

By the end of the 1980s, there was still no organizational theory of complexity, even in those streams that claimed to depart from the mainstream, and that pointed directly to complexity as an important theme. In 1989, under the title 'Toward an anthropology of complex organizations', Barbara Czarniawska, then Czarniawska-Joerges (1989) – who later became a household name in neo-institutional and cultural studies of organizations, stated that organizations were systems of collective action, and the contents of the action were meanings and things (ibid., p. 3). She claimed to adopt the American organizational psychologist Karl Weick's perspective on organizations as enacted and socially constructed (Weick, 1979). With regard to the word 'complex', she stated: 'Everybody knows that complex organizations are large and vice versa. . . . One can say that an organization becomes complex when no one can sensibly and comprehensibly account for the whole of it' (ibid., p. 6). She went on to refer to March and Simon (1958) to defend a view that organizations are hard to define because basically they are a result of human construction and our cultures.

Czarniawska-Joerges's rather evasive understanding of complexity was concurrent with that of other neo-institutional thinkers of the 1980s, including one of the pioneers to whom she refers, namely political scientist James G. March. By 1984, March had not changed his view on complexity in organizations much since the 1950s. He still talked about institutions and organizations in terms of systems and complexity as something not defined, which basically amounts to being synonymous with the contextual mess we experience as reality:

> The new institutionalism is often couched in terms of a contrast between the complexity of reality and the simplifications provided by existing theories, but theoretical research from an institutional perspective cannot involve the pursuit of enormous contextual detail.
>
> (March and Olsen, 1984, p. 747)

Herbert A. Simon, March's co-author of their 1958 book, made a clearer attempt to address complexity, but placed himself firmly within holistic systems theory:

> Roughly, by a complex system I mean one made up of a large number of parts that interact in a non-simple way. In such systems, the whole is more than the sum of the parts, not in an ultimate, metaphysical sense, but in the important pragmatic sense that, given the properties of the parts and the laws of their interaction, it is not a trivial matter to infer the properties of the whole. In the face of complexity, an in-principle reductionist may be at the same time a pragmatic holist.
>
> (Simon, 1962, p. 468)

Sixteen years later, when he wrote about his view on science in his Nobel Prize biographical (Simon, 1978), he still held the same dualistic stance – typical of the 'pragmatic holist':

> I have had two guiding principles – to work for the 'hardening' of the social sciences so that they will be better equipped with the tools they need for their difficult research tasks; and to work for close relations between natural scientists and social scientists so that they can jointly contribute their special knowledge and skills to those many complex questions of public policy that call for both kinds of wisdom.

Scholars, who in the 1950s were eager to establish a behavioural science for organizations, mobilized general systems thinking as a framework idea upon which to base this so-called science. In March and Simon's (1958) book, which became a kind of bible for organizational theory in political science and institutionalism, they sustained and amplified the idea of organizations and individuals as system levels with boundaries. Thus, the 1980s neo-institutionalism and cultural approaches to organizations were a mixture between the long-standing holistic systems idea from the 1950s and a constructivist idea that emerged in sociology in the 1960s, as exemplified in the widely cited book by Berger and Luckman (1966). These directions did not represent any progress with respect to the theme of complexity.

Group Behaviour

Another approach to organizational, psychological, and cultural studies of organizations started in the 1950s with attention to group behaviour and socialization (Homans, 1950; Jacques, 1951). Notably, organizational psychologist Edgar Schein studied how organizations influenced individuals in various contexts, ranging from psychological stress on American prisoners of war in the Korean War (Schein, 1957, 1961a) to changes of attitudes in institutional management education (Schein, 1961b). Later, he focused his research explicitly on organizational culture (Schein, 1985), which gained him international recognition in the 1980s' popularity wave on the same theme.

What from early on seemed to have occupied organizational researchers in the fields of organizational psychology, sociology, and cultural studies was the influence that organizations and groups have on individuals and, in turn, how individuals make sense of such experiences. The common challenge was to explain what happens between the individual and the organization, seen as two different levels of existence. The underlying idea remained of the organization as a system, an unclear and fuzzy collective in which individuals find themselves immersed. From this perspective, behaviour in organizations can no longer be fully attributed to individual choice because the system (i.e. organization) weighs so heavily on people's psyche. After having studied people under extreme stress, and reflecting on the collective communist paranoia in 1950s America, Schein wrote:

> It is no wonder that we have begun to question where the limits of the integrity of the human mind lie, and increasingly to entertain concepts like 'brainwashing' which expresses graphically our loss of confidence in our capacity as individuals to master our world.
>
> (Schein, 1959, p. 430)

Thirty years later, on the eve of Eastern Europe's totalitarian era, Czarniawska-Joerges, who herself was raised and educated in post-war totalitarian Poland, wrote: 'Organization is a system of collective action, undertaken in an effort to influence the world' (Czarniawska-Joerges, 1989, p. 3). One might think she was talking about communism and the way organized action deprives individuals of their capacity to act, much like Schein discussed earlier. However, Czarniawska-Joerges's idea was meant to be a definition of all kinds of organizations. The idea held no explanation of what a system is, what collective action is, or how a system is created or sustained as collective action by people. Furthermore, Czarniawska-Joerges did not explain what she meant by 'influencing the world'. Regarding the theme of complexity in organizations, her article introduced a special issue of a journal in which contributors argued that complexity should be taken seriously. Nonetheless, there was no idea of what complexity means, other than to say that complex organizations are large and presumably created by a 'system of collective action'.

True enough, highly conforming organizational practices, whether in a communist state or in industrial organizations, are often large in scale in terms of resources and number of employees. Moreover, the observed behaviour in conform organizations seems like collective action. However, in those kinds of organizations, every motivation of the ideologies underpinning them and every driving force behind organized actions is about *reducing* and *removing* variety and complexity and creating conforming practices. How then, can it be obvious that a large organization is complex? How can a complex organization be a 'system of collective action'?

The problem of definition became even shakier for Czarniawska-Joerges (1989, p. 6) when she wrote: 'The way out is then fuzzy edged concepts.' It seems that the way out of the problem was as unclear as the way into it. If the problem in organizational theory is to define and understand the very centre of interest – organizations – and if the theory is based on a taken-for-granted notion of organizations as systems, then the fundamental idea immediately creates a need to define a boundary between what belongs to the individual and what belongs to the organization, as well as what is situated between the organization and the wider organized activity in societies. The problem is 'biting its tail', as it is being created as a consequence of its baseline assumptions that the organization is a system.

Czarniawska-Joerges's approach to complexity and action in organizations is quite different from Schein's in that she portrays organizations and complexity as a result of a lifeless system of collective actions, whereas Schein is concerned with how the very idea of collective action deprives individuals of their capacity to see themselves as actors and masters of their own efforts. One may ask whether there is any place for human agency in a 'system of collective action'. Even though claiming to build on the work of Weick, Czarniawska-Joerges exposes a derailing away from Weick when it comes to the idea of complexity. Complexity becomes located as a characteristic of collective action in a dead system, whereas Weick, as a constructivist, locates both the roots of organizational complexity and the ability to deal with it in the relations between individuals in a group.

Weick rejects the idea that the organization exists as a system operating on people. Organizations are quite the opposite of that; they are social constructions or enactments in everyday actions (Weick, 1979). Despite coming from a different starting point, Weick shares Schein's concern about how individuals' ability to act in organizations is reduced by learned routines, power relations, and biased assumptions, especially under stress (Weick, 1993). However, although both Weick and Schein view the conformity of 'collective action' as a threat to the individual ability to act, they also see 'culture' as an opportunity for individuals in groups and organizations to perform complex actions. Culture is a blessing and a curse: it has the potential for facilitating incredibly complex co-operations, but it also has the potential to deprive individuals of their creative capacity. Thus, Weick and his colleagues end up calling for the dual actions of 'mindful' individuals in collective action (Weick et al., 1999), a split between the individual and the group found in systems thinking. Schein calls for 'leadership' (associated with the individual leader) in organizational cultures seen as systems (Schein, 1985). As shown in this chapter, even though organization theory has followed slightly different streams of systems thinking and approaches in psychology, political science, sociology, and cultural studies from the late 1950s to the late 1980s, there was no major progress or change in the understanding of complexity in organizations in that period.

References

Berger, P.L. & Luckmann, T. (1966). *The Social Construction of Reality: A Treatise in the Sociology of Knowledge*. New York: Penguin.
Czarniawska-Joerges, B. (1989). Preface: Toward an anthropology of complex organizations. *International Studies of Management & Organization* 19(3), pp. 3–15.
Eisenhower, D.D. (1961). *Farewell Address*. www.eisenhowerlibrary.gov/research/online-documents/farewell-address (accessed 5 October 2021).
Emery, F.E. & Thorsrud, E. (1969). *Form and Content in Industrial Democracy*. London: Tavistock Institute.
Forrester, J.W. (1961). *Industrial Dynamics*. Cambridge, MA: Productivity Press.
Forrester, J.W. (1969). *Urban Dynamics*. Portland, OR: Productivity Press.
Forrester, J.W. (1971). *World Dynamics*. Portland, OR: Productivity Press.
Heims, S.J. (1991). *The Cybernetics Group*. Cambridge, MA: MIT Press.
Homans, G. (1950). *The Human Group*. New York: Harcourt Brace Jovanovich.
Jacques, E. (1951). *The Changing Culture of a Factory*. London: Tavistock.
Keller, E.F. (2008). Organisms, machines, and thunderstorms: A history of self-organization, part one. *Historical Studies in the Natural Sciences* 38(1), pp. 45–75.
March, J.G. & Simon, H.A. (1958). *Organizations*. New York: John Wiley and Sons.
March, J.G. & Olsen, J.P. (1984). The new institutionalism: Organizational factors in political life. *The American Political Science Review* 78(3), pp. 734–749.
NASA (2008). *Langley Research Center's Contribution to the Apollo Program*. www.nasa.gov/centers/langley/news/factsheets/Apollo.html (accessed 20 July 2021).

National Geographic (n.d.). *Early Manned Spaceflight: Space Race.* www.nationalgeographic.com/science/article/early-manned-spaceflight/ (accessed 20 July 2021).

Perrow, C. (1984). *Normal Accidents: Living with High-Risk Technologies.* Princeton, NJ: Princeton University Press.

Pouvreau, D. (2009). *The Dialectical Tragedy of the Concept of Wholeness: Ludwig von Bertalanffy's Biography Revisited.* Litchfield Park, AZ: ISCE.

Schein, E.H. (1957). Reaction patterns to severe, chronic stress in American army prisoners of war of the Chinese. *Journal of Social Issues* 13(3), pp. 21–30.

Schein, E.H. (1959). Brainwashing and totalitarianization in modern society. *World Politics* 11(3), pp. 430–441.

Schein, E.H. (1961a). *Coercive Persuasion.* New York: Norton.

Schein, E.H. (1961b). Management development as a process of influence. *Industrial Management Review* 2, pp. 59–77.

Schein, E.H. (1985). *Organizational Culture and Leadership.* San Francisco, CA: Jossey-Bass.

Simon, H.A. (1962). The architecture of complexity. *Proceedings of the American Philosophical Society* 106, pp. 467–482.

Simon, H.A. (1978). *Herbert Simon: Biographical.* Nobel Prize Outreach. www.nobelprize.org/prizes/economic-sciences/1978/simon/biographical/ (accessed 5 July 2021).

Trist, E. & Bamforth, K.W. (1951). Some social and psychological consequences of the long wall method of coal getting. *Human Relations* 4, pp. 3–38.

Van Gigch, J.P. (1974). *Applied General Systems Theory.* New York: Harper & Row.

Weick, K.E. (1979). *The Social Psychology of Organization.* 2nd ed. New York: McGraw-Hill.

Weick, K.E. (1993). The collapse of sensemaking in organizations: The Mann Gulch disaster. *Administrative Science Quarterly* 38(4), pp. 628–652.

Weick, K.E., Sutcliffe, K.M. & Obstfeld, D. (1999). Organizing for high reliability: Processes of collective mindfulness. In: Sutton, R.I. & Staw, B.M. (eds.) *Research in Organizational Behavior.* Volume 21, pp. 81–123. Greenwich, CT: Elsevier Science/JAI Press.

4   The Origins of Complexity Theories in Organizations

Complexity Theories in the Natural Sciences

There is no straightforward link between physics, chemistry, living organisms, human life, and society. However, as I have shown in the Chapters 1–3, key ideas in organizational theory have for a long time made such connections between human society and classical mechanics (i.e. Taylorism), biology (i.e. open systems), and engineering (i.e. cybernetics). This foundation has crucially coloured the view of complexity in organizations because it places two fundamental beliefs as reference points for organizational evolution – one is that organizational change can be thought of in terms of *linearity*, and the other is that organizations can be seen in terms of *equilibrium*. Earlier in history, the questions that were pursued in the natural sciences on the basis of these two ideas meant that scientific discovery was all about finding eternal natural laws, repetitive patterns, and clear causal relationships, which in turn would make it possible to predict the future based on the past. Reality could be seen as 'time reversible' in the sense that causal relationships would be valid in exactly the same way, no matter which direction in time and space one would look. In the holistic open systems view there was a realization that equilibrium was problematic, but the view settled on the idea that equilibrium could be dynamic and held within operating boundaries by negative feedback loops, as described by cybernetics.

However, taking complexity seriously means endeavouring to explore questions about observable realities that are *not* in line with the assumptions that nature and society evolve as reversible processes, linearity, and equilibrium. From the 1960s, partly on the fringes of scientific research and partly in the political hotspot of the race between the superpowers United States and the Soviet Union, a new set of theories was emerging in the natural sciences and computer sciences, which in contrast to earlier theories investigated the dynamics of the phenomena of *non-linearity* and *non-equilibrium*.

DOI: 10.4324/9781003042501-5

Consequently, the new theories challenged the fundamental notions of reality as portrayed in the classical natural sciences, social sciences, economics, and organizational theory. In this chapter, the new theories will be referred to as *complexity theories.*

The Problem of Equilibrium in Nature

At the start of the 20th century, physicists thought that any chemical reaction and physical system would be either in a state of equilibrium with its environment or end up being in one. However, there were several problems with this explanation. Science historian Evelyn Fox Keller notes that at the time '[e]ntropy, organization, stability, equilibrium – all of these concepts raised immensely difficult problems for reconciling biological processes with the new science of thermodynamics' (Keller, 2009, p. 58).

The then new, but now classical, physics field of thermodynamics dealt with how energy flows and influences physical, chemical, and eventually biological processes. It was founded on three natural laws, two of which were formulated in the mid-19th century. The German physicist Hermann Helmholtz drew on earlier work by the French mechanical engineer Sadi Carnot, the English physicist James Prescott Joule, and others to formulate the first law of thermodynamics in 1847. The law stated the principle of conservation of energy: in an isolated system, energy cannot appear from nothing and disappear into nothing. The sum of all energy is a constant and can only be transformed into different types, such as mechanical movement, heat, chemical energy, or electricity.

The second law of thermodynamics evolved from several contributions. The first formulation is credited to the German physicist Rudolf Clausius in 1850 and was published in English in the following year (Clausius, 1851). The law stated that in an isolated system the degree of disorder, called entropy, is zero or increasing.

The German chemist Walther Nernst formulated the third law of thermodynamics at the beginning of the 20th century. It stated that the entropy or disorder of an isolated system is constant at absolute zero temperature (i.e. −273.15 °C). As entropy increases, the system is driven towards the minimum state of energy, which is equilibrium. Chemical reactions exchange energy in such a way that the resulting chemical compound is stabilized in equilibrium.

Whereas the three natural laws of thermodynamics assumed equilibrium, researchers in physical chemistry recognized that non-equilibrium conditions were important; they just did not have a feasible theory for how to understand such conditions in terms of the laws of thermodynamics.

Non-equilibrium thermodynamics remained a mystery until 1929, when the 26-year-old Norwegian chemical engineer Lars Onsager solved the problem of finding a mathematical theory of non-equilibrium chemical reactions.

Beyond Equilibrium

Onsager's theory of non-equilibrium chemical reactions was published in two groundbreaking papers (Onsager, 1931a, 1931b), for which in 1968 he won the Nobel Prize in Chemistry, for laying the mathematical groundwork that allowed a description of irreversible processes, and consequently our understanding of thermodynamics beyond equilibrium. In the same way as quantum physics had expanded beyond classical atomic physics, and relativity theory had expanded beyond classical mechanics, Onsager had expanded classical thermodynamics into the realm of non-equilibrium physics. He had strengthened the links between the three sciences of physics, chemistry, and biology, and thereby facilitated research in a direction towards a deeper understanding of the leap between the inanimate and the living world (i.e. the emergence of biological complexity in the natural world). The importance of the mathematical relations that is named Onsager's reciprocal relations is underlined by the fact that it is often referred to as the fourth law of thermodynamics. However, Onsager's work concerned near-equilibrium conditions, and there was still much work to be done for non-equilibrium physics.

In the first decades of the 20th century, physicists and biologists struggled with the fact that a living and seemingly self-sustaining entity such as a cell could come into existence from thermodynamical processes in which the energy transport seeks the least and most stable conditions. Why and how could structures such as a living cell and even more complex living structures such as animals and humans emerge in a nature that must obey a law of entropy (i.e. decay)?

On the one hand, the second law of thermodynamics tells us that order – life – is constantly falling apart and dying, while, on the other hand, life arises, is sustained, and keeps resisting the process of death in different temporal dimensions. Any living organism is organized on the basis of something that is not the organism itself, and any living organism eventually dies within relatively specific time frames. Additionally, there is an evolutionary process that operates beyond individual organisms' and species' lifespans and that adapts and sustains life in some form on our planet for a very long time. Not only that, it seems that in the longer time frame evolution creates increasingly complex and diverse forms of life. As time moves forward, the resistance against the entropy and decay dictated by the second law of thermodynamics seems to increase. How is this increasing complexity possible and explainable when classical thermodynamics tells us that the opposite should be happening?

The paradox of the biology of creation and the physics of decay, of life and death, was elaborated on by the Austrian quantum physics pioneer Erwin Schrødinger in his widely known book *What Is Life?* (Schrødinger, 1944) According to Schrödinger, the answer was negative entropy or 'negentropy' (ibid., p. 71). However, Schrødinger's explanation remained within the equilibrium thesis and still could not explain how something new and more complex could arise and become stabilized while entropy increased. Furthermore, he could not explain the role of non-equilibrium in such processes.

Schrødinger was an important contributor to quantum mechanics, which provided groundbreaking new insights into the physics of the atomic world. However, aligning quantum physics with non-equilibrium thermodynamics was far from a reality, and in his 1944 book with its ambitious title, Schrødinger seemed unaware of Onsager's breakthrough. He basically argued that biology could be explained from the statistical laws of classical thermodynamics and quantum physics. However, explaining how life could emerge from thermodynamics was beyond these explanations and still a mystery unsolved.

Far From Equilibrium

From the 1960s, the Belgian physical chemist Ilya Prigogine and his colleagues extended research on non-equilibrium thermodynamics to *far-from-equilibrium* conditions (Prigogine and Nicolis, 1967; Prigogine and Lefever, 1968). Prigogine knew Onsager's work and he himself had worked on the problems of irreversible processes and non-equilibrium since the 1940s (Prigogine, 1947, 1955). When investigating far-from-equilibrium conditions, Prigogine and his colleagues revealed astonishing results that would pave the way for a new understanding of complexity in nature (Prigogine and Stengers, 1984). The research won Prigogine the Nobel Prize for Chemistry in 1977.

Some of the results of Prigogine's research are summarized in his Nobel Lecture 'Time, structure and fluctuations' (Prigogine, 2012). In the lecture, he directed attention to the way he and others had expanded on Onsager's early work to a point where the understanding of the dynamics of the natural world was fundamentally altered. Furthermore, he explained how irreversible non-equilibrium processes (in which energy dissipates) paradoxically could become a source of a new type of dynamic state of matter, which he called *dissipative structures*. This understanding – that order can paradoxically emerge from non-equilibrium conditions in which, according to the second law of thermodynamics, order falls apart – is one of the foundational precepts in the development of a complexity paradigm of nature.

When Prigogine outlined the organizing principles of time, structure, and fluctuations in physical and mathematical terms he also included some of the fundamental ideas shaping a potentially radical new paradigm of social dynamics, given that the proposed ideas about nature have a counterpart in the organizational dynamics of the human world. In the statement from The Royal Swedish Academy of Sciences concerning its decision to award the Nobel Prize for Chemistry to Prigogine, the Academy hinted at the possible implications of his work for other sciences:

> The formation of ordered, dissipative systems demonstrates, however, that it is possible to create order from disorder. The description of these structures has led to many fundamental discoveries and applications in diverse fields of human endeavour, not only in chemistry. In the last few years, applications in biology have been dominating but the theory of dissipative structures has also been used to describe phenomena in social systems.
>
> (The Royal Swedish Academy of Sciences, 1977)

The insights from Prigogine's research became a cornerstone of what was later termed *the complexity sciences*. From the 1990s onwards, interpretations of the insights from the complexity sciences diffused into the field of organizational studies. This interest was further strengthened in the 2000s, not least due to the publication of Prigogine's bestselling popular scientific book *The End of Certainty* (Prigogine, 1997).

Prigogine and his colleagues demonstrated that the phenomenon of *self-organization* implies that structures and complexity emerge irreversibly in nature (Glansdorff and Prigogine, 1971; Nicolis and Prigogine, 1977). In his book, *The End of Certainty*, Prigogine (1997) argues that this insight has large consequences for our world view. He shows how non-linear interactions leads to self-organizing order or structure through minor fluctuations when ensembles of molecular structures (gases) are far from equilibrium, in a condition popularly known as the *edge of chaos*. There, the dissipative structures are formed from disorder, something that, according to traditional interpretations of the phenomenon of entropy in the second law of thermodynamics, should not happen. However, the second law turns out not to be violated by Prigogine's findings, because even if the sum of the entropy in the confined gas is zero or positive, negative entropy can emerge in the internal shifting (i.e. fluctuations) of movements in the gas or be imported into different areas of the gas as long as the gas is not confined.

The discovery that instability and irreversibility are fundamental measures in nature, and that they are foundations for spontaneous self-organizing emergence of order, points to other principles of causality than what proponents of systems thinking had been presenting earlier (Kondepudi et al., 2017). It means that *time* affects the connections in nature, which is another breach with traditional physics (Pagels, 1985). Usually, natural laws have been seen to operate independently of time, yet Prigogine and his co-researchers discovered that causes and effects in nature are affected by time. At some point, a structure can spontaneously self-organize into connections that have never been there before. Furthermore, stable connections might suddenly collapse. This finding characterizes the phenomenon of complexity and the meaning of irreversibility (Prigogine et al., 1972a, 1972b).

The Arrow of Time

The arrow of time means that, in the context of nature, structuration is dependent on time. Causes and effects break down and disappear over time, and what we think we see at one point in time will not necessarily always be the same in the future. In this regard, one can see here a dramatic break with the methodological foundation of the natural sciences with respect to causality. Prigogine's discoveries imply a different view of how nature evolves, and how the causes of this evolution are constructed (Prigogine, 1997).

Although natural laws have taught us about exact causalities independent of time and place, it is also clear that the most basic principle in nature is the uncertainty principle in quantum physics, which was defined by Heisenberg (1927). The principle states that certain pairs of physical quantities, such as the position and momentum of a particle, cannot be predicted precisely at the same time based on initial conditions. From the largest to the smallest scale, in nature as well as in society, reality is uncertain to the degree that if, in the natural sciences, one identifies causalities that are mathematically perfect, it will be because the type of phenomenon or the active agents involved in the relationship at hand have been isolated from respectively its or their natural context and their complex interactions in such a way that it is possible to measure particular and precise connections between cause and effect. This means that if conditions are kept the same in different experiments repeated several times in different places, the connection will be shown either to exist or not exist in the same way. If the same conditions are removed and left uncontrolled, as in the case of the natural world and human society, then the otherwise clear connection will be distorted and altered, and measurements will inevitably become diffuse and uncertain.

Heisenberg's uncertainty principle introduced a measurement problem in the physical world that led to the realization that it is impossible to measure precisely what is going on at the atomic and subatomic level. Therefore, quantum physics has to operate with *probabilities*. However, in quantum physics there is still the idea that time does not matter, while in nature the arrow of time means a different type of uncertainty. Prigogine's discoveries pointed to the structuring ability in irreversible processes in nature. This means that the physical future (nature) is unknown and unpredictable, and that structures will emerge that have not been there before. Uncertainty is not just a problem associated with measurement and probabilities of given outcomes as in classical physics and quantum physics; it is a consequence of time and the production of *possibilities* of outcomes never seen before. Hence, according to Prigogine, the laws of physics must be reformulated with this insight taken into account in order to understand the complexity in nature (Prigogine, 1997).

When complexity theory in organizations first became a hot topic in the 1990s, it was the work of Prigogine, through his 1977 Nobel Prize, and subsequent popular books (Prigogine, 1980, 1997), that became reference points for research on the wider importance of non-equilibrium physics and complexity. However, in the history of complexity in organizations, it is also important to note the fundamental work of Lars Onsager. Although rarely referred to in the context of organizations, it was Onsager's pioneering work that opened up the field of non-equilibrium physics. The difference between Onsager's results and Prigogine's results is that Onsager treated the conditions in near-equilibrium, where linearity still holds. Prigogine moved the focus to far-from-equilibrium or chaotic conditions, where non-linearity is the rule and linearity is the exception. The research interest into non-linearity in physical chemistry increased from the 1960s onwards, but it was not the only field in science in which chaotic phenomena and non-linearity was important. Understanding non-linear dynamics became crucial also in space flights and meteorology.

Non-linearity

In October 1957, the successful launching of the Soviet space craft Sputnik 1 perplexed the world, not least American scientists and engineers who had to realize that the United States' space technology was behind the Soviet's. The root of the problem was to be found in the differences in mathematical knowledge (Keller, 2009, p. 7). In the Soviet Union, mathematicians had long been occupied with problems of non-linear dynamics and control theory. However, in the West, not much attention had been paid to this development in mathematics. To have a rocket flying into space in a controlled way and then orbit around the Earth is not just a problem to do with building a rocket with the necessary engine power and capacity. It is equally a problem to do with stabilizing and bringing under control the extreme forces and non-linear disturbances that would otherwise cause the rocket to crash or fly off and out of its planned trajectory. The solution to the problem requires advanced non-linear mathematics and automated guiding systems. The launch of Sputnik 1 was a formidable victory for Soviet mathematicians, who in contrast to their counterparts in the United States had for a long time been systematically engaged in doing the groundwork for their own spectacular event. Keller notes that, as a consequence of the United States being mathematically blindsided, 'studies of nonlinear dynamical systems in the West exploded after 1960' (Keller, 2009, p. 7).

Already one month after the launch of Sputnik 1, the Russian-born American mathematician Solomon Lefschetz was mandated to establish a research centre based on industry and devoted to non-linear mathematics. Since World War II, Lefschetz had been familiar with the Soviet research. From 1946 until his retirement in 1953, he headed a research centre at Princeton University. However, after his retirement, the centre was closed down. Then, in the wake of the launch of Sputnik, he was called upon to revive the research on non-linear dynamical systems (Keller, 2009, p. 7).

By 1964, a massive programme to translate and make available Soviet research, previously largely unknown to US scientists, was launched by the large government agencies and industrial companies involved in the space programmes. According to Keller, by 1963 half of the references in a widely used textbook on the subject of stability theory were from Soviet publications (Cesari, 1963, cited in Keller, 2009, p. 7). In a NASA update of the book's reference list from 1965, the list was expanded by an additional 891 references, most of them from Soviet sources (Keller, 2009, p. 7).

Chaos

While researchers in the space programmes threw themselves into studies of non-linear dynamical systems, Edward Norton Lorenz, a mathematician and meteorologist working at the Department of Meteorology, MIT, wrote what would become a well-known paper, in which he presented his discovery that small changes in initial weather conditions would lead to larger changes in the weather in the long term (Lorenz, 1963). This indicated that atmospheric conditions needed to be represented by non-linear dynamic modelling, a discovery that often is referred to as the beginning of chaos theory, although the term chaos was not introduced in the research field until the mid-1970s (Li and York, 1975; Lorenz, 2005). Lorenz's groundbreaking discovery was initially largely ignored in science communities, perhaps because it seemed like a peculiar mathematical curiosity based on data from a very primitive computer device.

A decade after his discovery, Lorenz gave a talk at the 139th Meeting of the American Society for the Advancement of Science (Lorenz, 1972). To draw the audience's attention to his findings on sensitive dependence on initial conditions, and the fundamental impossibility and unpredictability of long-term weather forecasts, the talk was titled 'Predictability; does the flap of a butterfly's wings in Brazil set off a tornado in Texas?'

Lorenz's thought-provoking metaphor later became widely known as *the butterfly effect* through popular books such as one by Gleick (1987), and to this day the term serves as a metaphor for non-linearity and unpredictable surprises in both nature and society. The strength of the dependence on initial conditions in nature has since been much debated but the butterfly metaphor has been used not only in science and meteorology but also in economics, organizational studies, management, and popular culture.

According to Emmanuel (2011), Lorenz's discovery was the last nail in the coffin of the mechanical world view. Certainly, it was an important blow to the idea that linear causality in science could suffice in describing a complex reality, be it in nature or society. Theories describing phenomena of non-linear and chaotic behaviour in nature are today a fundamental part of complexity ideas in the natural sciences.

Complexity Theories in Organizational Research

As I have shown thus far in this first part of the book, there has been a long history of inspiration being drawn from the natural sciences by researchers working in the social and organizational sciences.

Since the 1990s, in the wake of the spread of popular literature that introduced to a wider audience the concepts of chaos and complexity in nature (Gleick, 1987; Waldrop, 1992), specific new understandings of complexity emerged in organizational theory. Complexity theories in organizational studies have since evolved in different directions. One early stream was based on ideas of organizations as *chaotic systems*. Then came the idea of organizations as *complex adaptive systems* (CAS), after which a theory emerged describing organizations as *complex responsive processes*.

The new generation of organizational theories differs from earlier theories in that they have strong links and take inspiration directly from phenomena that were discovered, explored, and explained by complexity research in the natural sciences, specifically the groundbreaking research into non-linear dynamics and non-equilibrium thermodynamics. In a much more specific way, the new theories address complexity as the key issue in organizations and therefore such theories can be named *organizational complexity theories*. In the natural sciences, complexity theories address how order and patterns can arise and collapse as a consequence of non-linear, self-organizing interaction processes in non-equilibrium conditions. Organizational complexity theories aim at exploring the meaning of such insights in organizations. The following sections present a short overview of the theories and their different understandings of complexity in organizations.

Organizations as Chaotic Systems

The interest in chaos theory in organizations started after James Gleick's bestselling popular science book titled *Chaos* drew widespread attention to the research field of chaos and complexity in nature (Gleick, 1987). The book tells the story of some of the people who pioneered the research on the mathematics and physics of non-linearity and chaos in nature, from Lorentz in the 1960s to the brilliant mathematician Mitchell Feigenbaum, who in the 1970s made the astonishing mathematical discovery of universal behaviour in non-linear systems (Feigenbaum, 1983). Feigenbaum worked at the Los Alamos National Laboratory in New Mexico, which was the site originally established for the first atomic bomb research – the Manhattan Project. Gleick's story recounts the struggle that Feigenbaum and other outstanding scientists engaged in to understand the nature of non-linearity and chaos, a field that for most scientists and mathematicians seemed impossible or even uninteresting to research.

An event that occurred in the same year as Gleick's book about chaos was published gave resonance to the title of the book in society. On 19 October 1987, a day later known as Black Monday, stock markets around the globe suddenly and unexpectedly collapsed. At the time, it was difficult to explain how the meltdown could have happened so abruptly and unforeseen. The collapse was just as hard to predict based on the trajectory of the markets before the breakdown and known parameters in economics, as it was to predict from meteorological data when a hurricane formed above oceans or a tornado formed in Texas. This raised the question of whether Lorenz's chaos theory was applicable to economics.

In the wake of the stock market crash, a more open globalized economic world emerged that was to dramatically change the meaning of 'organization'. The Soviet Union, along with former communist Eastern European countries, collapsed around 1990; China opened up for more trade relations after the brutal crackdown and massacre of protesters who were calling for democracy in Beijing's Tiananmen Square in 1989, and the European Union was formed in 1994. During the 1990s, the Internet became a communicative driving force in business and society. The emergence of globalism coincided with researchers' attention turning towards a paradigm shift in exploring the meaning of chaos and complexity in organizational studies. Economists, investment brokers, and business strategists took interest in the idea that chaos theory could be applied as a suitable way of describing and understanding the dynamics of markets and organizational realities (Kelsey, 1988; Peters, 1991, 1994). Among those who took inspiration from Gleick's book was the British economist Ralph D. Stacey. In the course of the next two decades Stacey made substantial contributions to the development of organizational complexity theory. His first ideas on the subject were published in a book titled *The Chaos Frontier: Creative Strategic Control for Business* (Stacey, 1991), which was followed by *Managing Chaos* (Stacey, 1992) and the first edition of a strategy textbook (Stacey, 1993). In subsequent editions of the textbook, Stacey moved away from chaos theory towards CAS theory (Stacey, 1996a), before eventually developing a new organizational complexity theory based on social theory (Stacey, 2001).

In addition to Stacey's books, many books and articles were published in the 1990s with the themes of chaos and complexity in the business domain. These included popular texts that told leaders about how to be successful in the age of knowledge, innovation, and complexity (Wheatley, 1992). The development reflected a growing fascination among organization and management scholars and consultants regarding how well the dynamic phenomena of complexity and chaos theory matched and potentially explained the new uncertain and hyperinteractive world of business and economy (Kellert, 1993; Thietart and Forgues, 1995).

However, by the mid-1990s, some researchers argued that chaos and complexity theories were premature in organizational contexts and that theorizing had not yet led to any clear differentiation between chaos and complexity (Begun, 1994). While complexity sciences in organizational studies seemed very promising, as a research field it lacked legitimacy. The instrumentalists in organizational research were asking for more rigorous modelling in accordance with systems theory (Casti, 1994; Allen, 1998), while the postmodernist and phenomenological theorists were asking for more critical contact with social theory, human processes, and postmodern philosophies (Cilliers, 1998; Dillon, 2000).

Organizations as Complex Adaptive Systems

Before Black Monday, some economists had already begun to take interest in what complexity would mean in economic terms. Since its start in 1984, The Santa Fe Institute had evolved into a hub for theories of, and experiments with, complex adaptive systems. Economist W. Brian Arthur recalls that his interest started when he and his colleagues arranged a workshop at the Santa Fe Institute in September 1987 (Jaworski et al., 1999). The workshop was followed in 1988 by a research programme, which was financially supported by Citibank. According to Arthur, Citibank gave him and his colleagues a free hand to explore what it meant to see the economy as a complex adaptive systems. Their research resulted in several publications, among them Arthur's articles on the consequences of complexity thinking for economics, technological development, and innovation (Arthur, 1989, 1996). Over the years, this stream of research constituted an alternative school to traditional economic theory under the term *complexity economics* (Arthur, 2014).

The CAS-related research investigated the emergence of increasing degrees of complexity by studying the interaction dynamics of independent actors in networks. The phenomenon of interest was *self-organization*. With the help of advanced computer modelling, the focus of investigations was on understanding the local interactions between agents that were not guided by any overall programme for the agents' behaviour (Holland, 1998).

In CAS thinking, the idea of *equilibrium* and *controllable wholes*, which is crucial in general systems theory, was abandoned, while the notion of systems was kept. According to the CAS way of thinking, systems are abstract structures that unpredictably emerge as a result of the interactions of agents in dynamic patterns without an overall structural plan. CAS thinkers do not differentiate between social structure as a continuous production of what interacting people are doing and the patterns that their interactions produce. A pattern is a system, and the dynamics of a pattern is the adaptive process of the system in which a new system is created. Complex adaptive systems generate more complex adaptive systems (Gell-Mann, 1994).

Characteristic of a CAS is that it includes a medium number of individual agents with only local and limited information. The agents in the computer model are intelligent in the sense that they are capable of adapting to their local environment. The idea that one can model and simulate complexity has led researchers to start talking about phenomena in organizations as if they are the same as the phenomena they see in the computer models. Casti (1994) and Wolfram (2002) argued that computers made it possible to test theories of what he called social and behavioural systems. However, Lissack and Richardson (2001, p. 98) strongly critiqued Casti's and Wolfram's simplified understanding of complexity in general and social complexity and people in particular:

> Merely to study models – without concern for the observed or the modeled – suggests a positivistic belief in the powers of prediction and self-fulfilling cause that are foolish when applied to the 'natural sciences' and dangerous when applied to the social sciences.
>
> Wolfram has become the most recent, and John Casti perhaps the most vigorous, proponent of the misconception that the study of models is the study of people.

Researchers within the CAS direction of organizational research argued the importance of complexity in organizational studies as being firmly based on the natural sciences and that CAS theory, if kept in line with its natural scientific roots, provided a solid foundation for management studies (Anderson, 1999; Maguire and McKelvey, 1999; McKelvey, 1999). The assumption was that human organizations are literally CAS (Sanders, 1998; Pascale et al., 2000; Uhl-Bien et al., 2007). However, Stacey argued that organizational complexity studies should be grounded in social theory rather than in the natural sciences. He had moved from seeing organizations as chaotic systems in the early 1990s (Stacey, 1991) to seeing organizations as CAS in the mid-1990s (Stacey, 1996b). Then, at the end of the1990s, he also departed from that idea towards a theory describing organized activity as *complex responsive processes of relating*. It was a theory that rejected all organizational theories that were based directly on the language and concepts of systems and models, including CAS (Stacey, 2001).

These emerging ideas were subsequently more fully developed in several books that were published up until 2010 (e.g. Stacey, 2005, 2010; Stacey and Griffin, 2005). The two theoretical foundations of CAS and complex responsive processes are different directions in organizational complexity research, depending on whether one holds the view that all sciences should be based on the *same* ontological and epistemological criteria or on different criteria (see Chapter 5, for more on this discussion).

Organizations as Complex Responsive Processes

In the theory of complex responsive processes (Stacey et al., 2000; Stacey, 2001), Stacey invoked the thinking of the American pragmatist philosopher George Herbert Mead and the German sociologist Norbert Elias in developing a social theory of complexity. Stacey also drew on ideas from the complexity sciences as analogous in describing organizational dynamics. Mead and Elias seem to have shared an ontological view of time, space, and experience with the view that Prigogine (1997) had presented based on studies of irreversibility and complexity in nature. Prigogine claimed that nature and society move in time and space according to the same kind of causality principle that Stacey (2001) termed *transformative causality*. At the same time, Stacey harshly critiqued systems thinking, which in contrast to his theory of complex responsive processes, assumed that movement happened according to the rationalistic and formative causality principles as formulated by the German philosopher Immanuel Kant (see Chapter 5, for more discussion on causality and philosophy).

In complex responsive processes theory, human reality is not seen in terms of systems. Instead, it is seen as that which people enact to create their individual and social identity in communicative interaction with other people and environments. These processes are temporal and unpredictable, although pockets of stability in time and space are a feature of such volatile processes. Stacey (2010) argued that established systems theories (open systems) could not explain change and novelty. This can be exemplified by the idea of self-organizing, which in systems theories is thought of as producing ever-higher levels of a whole. Stacey holds that this does not bring anything new to the understanding of organizational reality and does not take seriously the radical new paradigm of complexity. Systems theories just incorporate complexity into the same way of thinking as if complexity were not present. Stacey's alternative approach is to think about self-organizing processes not as producing higher levels in systems but as the very centre of movement and iteration of reality in nature and society. Self-organizing processes do not produce anything other than further self-organizing processes, which are the interaction patterns between living entities, including humans, in a never-ending process of repetition and change.

Stacey claimed that human interaction bears no resemblance to systems. Even if we can theorize that objects and nature are different from humans in character and features, any relationship humans might engage in with objects and nature are still aspects of human interaction. Thus, proponents of systems thinking have not succeeded in developing a proper theory of human and social complexity because systems models, by definition, are simplifications and reifications of reality. By contrast, complexity is ingrained in every aspect of natural and human activity. Complexity views of reality challenge traditional science and present to us the limits to what the human mind can grasp, and certainly to what humans can control. In our endeavours to understand the realities in which we all exist, we are confronted not only with complexity but also with our own human limitations. This is a realization that nature and humans have emerged and will continue to emerge beyond human understanding and control.

Stacey argued that systems thinking is only one way of thinking about human stability and change and that clearly it can be substituted with forms of complexity thinking departing from systems theory to explain organizational and social reality in terms of what he termed complex responsive processes. Mead's theory of communication as a social interaction is the basis of how Stacey understood stability and change in organizations and societies.

Comparison of Organizational Complexity Theories

The 1990s and the first years of the new millennium were in a sense a golden age of theorizing complexity in organizational studies (Johannessen and Kuhn, 2012). Complexity thinking had by then become fairly well recognized as having a place in the landscape of approaches in organizational studies. Many scholars and practitioners were joining the discourse and using the ideas in different ways to understand various problems and phenomena in organized life. Also, important critique emerged. In particular, it became increasingly clear that CAS thinking and the theory of complex responsive processes moved in very different directions.

Stacey (2001) noted that computer models designed by programmers to simulate CAS are inappropriate to understand human organization, even though they are programmed to have their algorithms describe evolving interaction. A computer simulation is an oversimplification. In organizations, many people interact and converse with colleagues, customers, and others in a range of different contexts, including engaging in advanced knowledge work and innovation based on accumulated experience and judgement. Clearly, a computer model cannot encompass this human dynamics and complexity.

At a technical level, a computer simulation can show the emergence of interactional patterns, but humans in organizations do not behave in the same manner as a CAS that is being modelled by a computer. The richness of human interactive behaviour, feelings, and motives cannot be captured, although particular behavioural patterns in strictly regulated contexts, such as the directed movements of customers in a shop or crowds in a football stadium, can be simulated for the purpose of influencing shopping behaviour or crowd control. Moreover, CAS theory does not break the fundamental ties with earlier systems theories, although it unravels important phenomena and dynamics that are not treated in traditional systems thinking, and thereby it directs attention towards phenomena of complexity (Holland, 2006).

Nevertheless, theories of CAS and complex responsive processes share some common conceptual ground and pose similar challenges to mainstream organizational theory and management thinking. Complexity thinkers in both 'camps' view the future state of organizations as arising from evolving processes, the 'trajectories' of which play out over an extended period. These processes may be influenced, but not predicted. By contrast, mainstream organizational thinking conceives the future state of an organization as arising from a chain of more or less discreet events and management interventions, in which a high degree of predictability and control is not only possible but also essential.

The primary difference between the two streams of complexity thinking in organizational studies is that in complex responsive process theory it is argued that complexity concepts drawn from the physical sciences and mathematics are best viewed as analogies. They open the possibility for understanding organizations and organizational life as complex phenomena, but the direct application of these concepts to human action can only be done with great care and thoughtful interpretation. The CAS stream of thinking and research is based on the view that organizations behave in the same way as CAS. Hence, this way of thinking justifies that CAS theory and other concepts from the natural sciences and mathematics can be either applied directly to human action and management practice or interpreted as metaphors in order to understand complexity in organizations.

References

Allen, P.M. (1998). Evolving complexity in social science. In: Altman, G. & Koch, W.A. (eds.) *Systems: New Paradigms for the Human Sciences*, pp. 3–38. Berlin: Walter de Gruyter.

Anderson, P. (1999). Complexity theory and organization science. *Organization Science* 10, pp. 216–232.

Arthur, W.B. (1989). Competing technologies, increasing returns, and lock-in by historical events. *The Economic Journal* 99, pp. 116–131.

Arthur, W.B. (1996). Increasing returns and the new world of business. *Harvard Business Review* 74(4), pp. 100–109.

Arthur, W.B. (2014). *Complexity and the Economy*. Oxford: Oxford University Press.

Begun, J.W. (1994). Chaos and complexity: Frontiers of organization science. *Journal of Management Inquiry* 3(4), pp. 329–335.

Casti, J. (1994). *Complexification: Explaining a Paradoxical World through the Science of Surprise*. London: HarperCollins.

Cesari, L. (1963). *Asymptotic Behaviour and Stability Problems in Ordinary Differential Equations*. 2nd ed. Berlin: Springer-Verlag.

Cilliers, P. (1998). *Complexity and Postmodernism: Understanding Complex Systems*. London: Routledge.

Clausius, R. (1851). On the moving force of heat, and the laws regarding the nature of heat itself which are deducible therefrom. *London, Edinburgh, and Dublin Philosophical Magazine and Journal of Science, Series 4* 2(VIII), pp. 1–21, 102–119.

Dillon, M. (2000). Poststructuralism, complexity and poetics. *Theory, Culture & Society* 17(5), pp. 1–26.

Emmanuel, K. (2011). *Edward Norton Lorenz 1917–2008: A Biographical Memoir*. Washington, DC: National Academy of Sciences.

Feigenbaum, M.J. (1983). Universal behavior in nonlinear systems. *Physica 7*, pp. 16–39.

Gell-Mann, M. (1994). *The Quark and the Jaguar: Adventures in the Simple and the Complex*. New York: W.H. Freeman.

Glansdorff, P. & Prigogine, I. (1971). *Thermodynamic Theory of Structure, Stability and Fluctuations*. New York: John Wiley.

Gleick, J. (1987). *Chaos: Making of a New Science*. New York: Viking Penguin.

Heisenberg, W. (1927). Uber den anschaulichen Inhalt der quantentheoretischen Kinematik und Mechanik. *Zeitschrift for Physik* 43, pp. 172–198.

Holland, J.H. (1998). *Emergence: From Chaos to Order*. New York: Oxford University Press.

Holland, J.H. (2006). Studying complex adaptive systems. *Journal of Systems Science and Complexity* 19, pp. 1–8.

Jaworski, J., Jusela, G. & Scharmer, C.O. (1999). *Conversation with W. Brian Arthur Xerox Parc, Palo Alto, California*, 16 April. www.dialogueonleadership.org/ (accessed 15 June 2021).

Johannessen, S.O. & Kuhn, L. (eds.) (2012). *Complexity in Organization Studies*. Four-volume set. London: SAGE.

Keller, E.F. (2009). Organisms, machines, and thunderstorms: A history of self-organization, part two: Complexity, emergence, and stable attractors. *Historical Studies in the Natural Sciences* 39(1), pp. 1–31.

Kellert, S.H. (1993). *In the Wake of Chaos*. Chicago, IL: University of Chicago Press.

Kelsey, D. (1988). The economics of chaos or the chaos of economics. *Oxford Economic Papers* 40, pp. 1–31.

Kondepudi, D., Petrosky, T. & Pojman, J.A. (2017). Dissipative structures and irreversibility in nature: Celebrating 100th birth anniversary of Ilya Prigogine (1917–2003). *Chaos* 27, Article 104501.

Li, T.Y. & York, J.A. (1975). Period three implies chaos. *American Mathematical Monthly* 82(10), pp. 985–992.

Lissack, M.R. & Richardson, K.A. (2001). When modeling social systems, models ≠ the modeled: Reacting to Wolfram's *A New Kind of Science*. *Emergence* 3(4), pp. 95–111.

Lorenz, E.N. (1963). Deterministic nonperiodic flow. *Journal of the Atmospheric Sciences* 20, pp. 130–141.

Lorenz, E.N. (1972). *Predictability: Does the Flap of a Butterfly's Wings in Brazil Set Off a Tornado in Texas?* American Association for the Advancement of Science, 139th Meeting. https://eapsweb.mit.edu/sites/default/files/Butterfly_1972. pdf (accessed 2 September 2021).

Lorenz, E.N. (2005). Designing chaotic models. *Journal of the Atmospheric Sciences* 62, pp. 1574–1587.

Maguire, S. & McKelvey, B. (1999). Complexity and management: Moving from fad to firm foundations. *Emergence* 1(2), pp. 19–61.

McKelvey, B. (1999). Complexity theory in organization science: Seizing the promise or becoming a fad. *Emergence* 1(1), pp. 5–33.

Nicolis, G. & Prigogine, I. (1977). *Self-Organization in Nonequilibrium Systems: From Dissipative Structures to Order through Fluctuations*. New York: John Wiley & Sons.

Onsager, L. (1931a). Reciprocal relations in irreversible processes. I. *Physical Review* 37(4), pp. 405–426.

Onsager, L. (1931b). Reciprocal relations in irreversible processes. II. *Physical Review* 38(12), pp. 2265–2279.

Pagels, H.R. (1985). Is the irreversibility we see a fundamental property of nature? *Physics Today* 38(1), pp. 97–99.

Pascale, R.T., Millemann, M. & Gioja, L. (2000). *Surfing the Edge of Chaos: The Laws of Nature and the New Laws of Business*. New York: Crown Business.

Peters, E.E. (1991). *Chaos and Order in the Capital Markets*. New York: John Wiley.

Peters, E.E. (1994). *Fractal Market Analysis: Applying Chaos Theory to Investment and Economics*. New York: John Wiley.

Prigogine, I. (1947). *Etude thermodynamique des phénomènes irréversibles*. Liege: Desoer.

Prigogine, I. (1955). *Introduction to Thermodynamics of Irreversible Processes*. Springfield, IL: Charles C. Thomas.

Prigogine, I. (1980). *From Being to Becoming: Time and Complexity in the Physical Sciences*. San Francisco, CA: W.H. Freeman.

Prigogine, I. (1997). *The End of Certainty: Time, Chaos and the New Laws of Nature*. New York: The Free Press.

Prigogine, I. (2012). Time, structure and fluctuations. In: Johannessen, S.O. & Kuhn, L. (eds.) *Complexity in Organization Studies*. Volume 1, pp. 3–28. London: SAGE.

Prigogine, I. & Lefever, R. (1968). Symmetry breaking instabilities in dissipative systems. II. *The Journal of Chemical Physics* 48(4), pp. 1695–1700.

Prigogine, I. & Nicolis, G. (1967). On symmetry-breaking instabilities in dissipative systems. *The Journal of Chemical Physics* 46(9), pp. 3542–3550.

Prigogine, I. & Stengers, I. (1984). *Order Out of Chaos: Man's New Dialogue with Nature*. New York: Bantam Books.

Prigogine, I., Nicolis, G. & Babloyantz, A. (1972a). Thermodynamics of evolution. *Physics Today* 25(11), pp. 23–28.

Prigogine, I., Nicolis, G. & Babloyantz, A. (1972b). Thermodynamics of evolution. *Physics Today* 25(12), pp. 38–44.

The Royal Swedish Academy of Sciences (1977). The Nobel Prize in chemistry 1977. *Press Release*. www.nobelprize.org/prizes/chemistry/1977/press-release (accessed 12 October 2021).

Sanders, T.I. (1998). *Strategic Thinking and the New Science: Planning in the Midst of Chaos, Complexity, and Change*. New York: The Free Press.

Schrödinger, E. (1944). *What Is Life? The Physical Aspect of the Living Cell & Mind and Matter*. Cambridge: Cambridge University Press.

Stacey, R.D. (1991). *The Chaos Frontier: Creative Strategic Control for Business*. Oxford: Butterworth Heinemann.

Stacey, R.D. (1992). *Managing Chaos*. London: Kogan Page.

Stacey, R.D. (1993). *Strategic Management and Organisational Dynamics: The Challenge of Complexity*. 1st ed. London: Pearson Education.

Stacey, R.D. (1996a). *Strategic Management and Organisational Dynamics: The Challenge of Complexity*. 2nd ed. London: Pearson Education.

Stacey, R.D. (1996b). *Complexity and Creativity in Organizations*. San Francisco, CA: Berret-Koehler.

Stacey, R.D. (2001). *Complex Responsive Processes in Organizations: Learning and Knowledge Creation*. London: Routledge.

Stacey, R.D. (2005). *Experiencing Emergence in Organizations: Local Interaction and the Emergence of Global Pattern*. London: Routledge.

Stacey, R.D. (2010). *Complexity and Organizational Reality: Uncertainty and the Need to Rethink Management after the Collapse of Investment Capitalism.* London: Routledge.

Stacey, R.D. & Griffin, D. (2005). *Taking Experience Seriously: A Complexity Perspective on Researching Organizations.* London: Routledge.

Stacey, R.D., Griffin, D. & Shaw, P. (2000). *Complexity and Management: Fad or Radical Challenge to Systems Thinking?* London: Routledge.

Thietart, R.A. & Forgues, B. (1995). Chaos theory and organization. *Organization Science* 6, pp. 19–31.

Uhl-Bien, M., Marion, R. & McKelvey, B. (2007). Complexity leadership theory: Shifting leadership from the industrial age to the knowledge era. *Leadership Quarterly* 18(4), pp. 298–318.

Waldrop, M.M. (1992). *Complexity. The Emerging Science at the Edge of Order and Chaos.* New York, NY: Simon & Shuster.

Wheatley, M. (1992). *Leadership and the New Science.* San Francisco, CA: Berrett-Koehler.

Wolfram, S. (2002). *A New Kind of Science.* Champaign, IL: Wolfram Media.

Part 2

Philosophy, Science, and Organizational Practice

5 Complexity, Philosophy, and Social Theory

The Natural Sciences and the Human Sciences

In the 1930s, the American sociologist Herbert Blumer described two contrasting orientations in the methodological debate between social researchers in the United States, one being the stimulus–response approach and the other interactionism (Blumer, 1937). Researchers following the stimulus–response direction argued that the social sciences should favour objective data for quantitative analysis, like the psychological experimentation of instrumental behaviourism (Watson, 1913; Pavlov, 1927), with its clear basis in mechanistic natural science.

By contrast, researchers in the interactionist camp identified their basic unit of research as *human action*, thus bringing personal and social experiences to the attention of research. In an appraisal of the latter, Blumer argued that experiential data are valuable in the social sciences. Records of experience are important ways of gaining insights into a process of change 'here and now', although they do not meet the standard criteria of conventional natural science.

Blumer took inspiration from American philosophical pragmatism, particularly George Herbert Mead. Although the pragmatist philosophy disappeared into the margins of social theory after World War II (Joas and Knöbl, 2009), Blumer's version of pragmatism survived in the form of *symbolic interactionism* (Blumer, 1969).

The polarized methodological debate in social sciences that Blumer pointed to reflected a long-term stand off and confrontation between rationalism and empiricism. Rationalism in the tradition initiated by the French mathematician and philosopher René Descartes in the 16th century and solidified throughout the 17th century by the German mathematician and philosopher Gottfried Wilhelm Leibnitz, English mathematician and physicist Isaac Newton, and other contemporaries strongly emphasized the detached and objective researcher observing and formulating the mechanical

DOI: 10.4324/9781003042501-7

laws of nature and the universe. The counterstream of empiricism, as outlined in the 18th century by the Scottish philosopher David Hume (1978 [1740]), claimed that knowledge is subjectively constructed, relative, unreliable, and only reflects habits of thought and behaviour rather than the reality of nature.

In the late 18th century, the German philosopher Immanuel Kant attempted to synthesize Descartes's rationalism and Hume's empiricism in an explanation that held that nature and humans are guided by a *dual* causality principle. It was this thinking that gained support in many intellectual areas in the 19th and 20th centuries, including the emerging social sciences and eventually their influence in organizational studies (Stacey, 2001; Griffin, 2002).

Kantian Dualism

Although Kant had as his starting point Hume's prioritizing of the subjective autonomous human, he was critical of the notion of purely subjective constructed truth. However, he was also critical of the way deterministic scientific rationality did not attribute any significance to human free will. Rather, his suggestion was that there is a fixed reality beyond our reach, which individuals can only perceive as imperfect and variable. Whenever individuals do this, reality will appear to become relative. Kant referred to this duality as *Das Ding an sich* – the thing, or nature of things, which in itself is independent of human observation, and *Das Ding für mich* – the things as they appear to be in human sensation or experience. Thus, according to Kant, there is a given reality of nature, which our senses can come closer to experiencing but will never really comprehend because it transcends human possibilities of knowing. Our experience is limited as an instrument to understand nature (i.e. the complexity of nature).

Kant thought that when nature unfolds and change, it is because some characteristics are enfolded in it from the beginning, thus forming nature's evolution in particular ways. The internal interactions of nature's components are such that they produce more mature (i.e. complex) forms of whole organisms, clearly recognizable and predictable in their natural form (i.e. humans, animals, trees) but also clearly unpredictable and different as individual organisms.

However, Kant also claimed that when *human actions* evolve, it is because people make rational choices based on their individual free will. Hence, human causality is rational, while nature's causality is formative and based on pregiven characteristics. The full scale of reality evolves according to dualistic causality principles: human's rational causality (agency) and nature's formative causality. Kant's dualism implies that nature has a given purpose (teleology), whereas humans choose their purpose. The theory seeks both to explain and to defend a causal split between nature and humans as a legitimate reason for bridging both reliable scientific objectivity and unreliable human subjectivity.

After World War II, the social sciences moved away from the pre-war polarizing debate that Blumer had described in the late 1930s, and in a peculiar way adopted the Kantian 'bridge' – the dualistic logic of nature and humans – in order to explain the relationship between the subjective individual and the objective structure of society. In social theory, the American sociologist Talcott Parsons constructed a synthesis of the views of whom he thought had been the four most influential sociologists up until then, namely Emile Durkheim (French), Max Weber (German), Vilfredo Pareto (Italian), and T.H. Marshall (English). All four had made crucial contributions to the problem of emergence of social order, leading to the formulation of a kind of unified theory of social structure.

However, in his book *The Structure of Social Action* Parsons completely ignored the work of the American pragmatists (Parsons, 1937). As Parsons became a dominant figure in social theory in the 1940s and 1950s, pragmatist thinking more or less disappeared in social theory (Joas and Knöbl, 2009). Parsons's ideas were clearly in the neighbourhood of holistic systems theory (see Chapter 1). Hence, the dominance of a dualistic synthesis and the structuralist view both coincided with and influenced the rise of postwar organizational theory and eventually its view on complexity.

Thus, modern social sciences adopted the Kantian dualism, both in the version of Parsons's structuralism and in holistic systems thinking. The long-term influence of Kant was also expressed in philosophy and methodology. In the 19th century, thinkers such as the German philosopher and historian Wilhelm Dilthey had made connections between holistic ideas and *hermeneutics* in arguing that *meaning* emerges between the parts and the whole in a hermeneutical (i.e. interpretative) way. Thus, he suggested an interaction between separated levels of existence – the individual and the group/society.

In the 20th century, the German philosopher Martin Heidegger in his seminal work *Being and Time* (Heidegger, 1962) synthesized phenomenology and hermeneutics as an expression of neo-Kantianism. Another German philosopher, Hans-Georg Gadamer, in his grand work *Wahrheit und Methode*, first published in 1960 and later translated into English with the title *Truth and Method* (Gadamer, 2013), provided a further clarification of these ideas in order to explain that truth and method in the sciences are at odds with each other and that understanding (*Verstehen*) emerges as a mutual and dialogical interaction between persons or a person and a text or object of art.

Hence, Kantian dualism prevailed in a range of areas of philosophy and social theory throughout the 20th century, even though it did not take into account insights gained from the natural sciences from the mid-19th century and the early decades of the 20th century (insights that were central to the pragmatists). Charles Darwin had shown that nature does not evolve according to the Kantian theory of pregiven characteristics, while physics and chemistry had narrowed the gap to biology through non-equilibrium thermodynamics (see Chapter 4). Both of these fundamental insights were in direct opposition to the formative causality of Kantian dualism.

Objectivity in the Human Sciences

Around the mid-19th century, the French philosopher August Comte formulated the idea of *positivism* as the basis for social science. He argued for a *unified science*, in which the method in natural science (physics) should be exported to research on social and human issues. The idea of a unified science inspired the Austrian physicist Ernst Mach's description of *logical positivism* as characteristic of the natural scientific method, a view that into the 20th century influenced people such as Ludwig von Bertalanffy, who adopted the idea of a unity of science when he promoted his general systems theory (Bertalanffy, 1950, 1951). Even though Bertalanffy argued for a unity of science, he stated that there must be separate sets of laws for the natural and social sciences due to the major differences between the natural and social world. It was rather the prospect of his general systems theory and its structural generality that he promoted as a unifying framework for all sciences (Bertalanffy, 1968, pp. 86–88). The argument of how natural and human sciences needed to be brought together was also raised by the British scientist and novelist C.P. Snow in his widely discussed 1959 lecture 'The two cultures' (Snow and Collini, 1993, pp. 1–52), coincidently published at the same time as arguments of a general systems theory began to take hold in social sciences and organizational studies in particular.

However, despite the calls for unification, a fundamental problem in the social sciences, compared to the natural sciences, is the status of the observer and the participant, and the claim for objectivity in research. The first to unravel the methodological core of the problem and discuss it in depth was the Norwegian philosopher Hans Skjervheim, in his 1959 thesis titled 'Objectivism and the study of man', which was later published as two articles (Skjervheim, 1974a, 1974b). He argued that people cannot help being both observers and participants, but that positivistic science only acknowledges one of them, namely that of the observer.

In Skjervheim's view, there cannot be observation without participation and conversely there cannot be participation without observation; thus, to separate the two is meaningless when researching human affairs. However, he made a distinction between two basic attitudes in intersubjective communication – one is that of the observer who takes an objectivating attitude and the other is that of the participant who takes a performative attitude. If understanding (*Verstehen*) is the same as the observed objectified meaning agreed upon, and at the same time such objective meaning requires a participative process of reaching this understanding, then there is a fundamental problem in the social sciences to do with the validity claims of these sciences. If what the social scientist observes, and the reaching of meaning of what is observed are different processes – one detached, and the other involved – then objectivity becomes both possible and impossible at the same time, and hence, validity claims in the social sciences are at best problematic.

Jürgen Habermas, one of the most influential German philosophers and social theorists of the late 20th and early 21st century, referred to Skjervheim's discussion (Habermas, 1984, pp. 111–115) when he expanded the debate on the topic of the nature of knowledge and understanding (*Verstehen*) in the natural and human sciences in his major two-volume work *The Theory of Communicative Action* (Habermas, 1984, 1987). Habermas pointed out that Skjervheim was overlooked as 'the one who had first worked out the methodologically shocking consequences of what is problematic about *Verstehen*' (Habermas, 1984, p. 111).

Habermas and Verstehen

For Habermas, the main goal of the human and social sciences is to understand rather than to discover or explain anything in the form of a scientific law. He draws a historical line to neo-Kantian philosophers in his reasoning about understanding and truth in the social sciences:

> In the tradition stemming from Dilthey and Husserl, understanding (*Verstehen*) has been characterized *ontologically* by Heidegger in *Being and Time* as a basic feature of human existence, and reaching understanding (*Verständigung*) by Gadamer in *Truth and Method* as a basic feature of historical life. It is not at all my intention to rely systematically on this approach, but I would like to point out that the *methodological* discussions of recent decades concerning the foundations of the social sciences have led to similar results.
>
> (Habermas, 1984, p. 107)

Habermas's claim about truth has consequences for method and research in the social sciences:

There can be no universal standards of rationality claimed. Alternative standards exist with context dependent criteria. Consequence: Truth is not universal, but local. Truth is not relative in the sense that it is subjective. But it is intersubjective and context dependent.

(Habermas, 1984, pp. 58–59)

According to the British sociologist Anthony Giddens, *Verstehen* is not a method or particularity of the social sciences but a basic condition of human society:

> The generation of descriptions of acts of everyday actors is not incidental to social life as ongoing Praxis but is absolutely integral to its production and inseparable from it, since the characterization of what others do, and more narrowly their intentions and reasons for what they do, is what makes possible the intersubjectivity through which the transfer of communicative intent is realized. It is in these terms that *Verstehen* must be regarded: not as a special method of entry to the social world peculiar to the social sciences, but as the ontological condition of human society as it is produced and reproduced by its members.
>
> (Giddens, 1976, p. 151)

Habermas distinguishes between the natural and the social world, and he claims that in both domains it is possible to state facts and truths, but these are different dependent on the basic attitude taken towards the natural and social world. He also claims that we can become aware of this distinction of our attitude towards nature and towards society when we move from observing and doing things with objects to doing things in relation to the expectations from other people in our society:

> We make the correct conceptual separations between causal connections of nature and normative orders of society to the extent that we become conscious of the changes in perspective and attitude that we effect when we pass from observing or manipulating to following or violating legitimate expectations.
>
> (Habermas, 1984, p. 49)

Habermas criticizes how rationality has taken a universal form in modern society and thereby hindered a distinction between the natural and the cultural world. This fusion is no different from the mediaeval magical mythical fusion wherein humans did not understand themselves as individuals capable of detaching themselves from nature, and not able by reflexive thinking to detach themselves from their own existence, to see themselves as an object in the world. Rather, they saw themselves as creatures immersed in the world of supernatural spirits where they were unable to take any control of their own destiny (Habermas, 1984, p. 44). This universality, Habermas claims, has led to confusion between the physical and the moral domain, and a lack of differentiation between them.

The Habermas–Luhmann Debate

Although arguing for differentiation in line with Kantian dualism, and at the same time drawing influence from systems theory, Habermas came to distance himself from the more radical defenders of holistic systems theory, such as his fellow countryman and sociologist Niklas Luhmann, whom he clashed with and became the most important opponent of, as Luhmann's systems thinking grew in popularity during the 1970s. For a detailed discussion of the Habermas–Luhmann debate, see Harste (2021).

Habermas argued for a restoration of the values and tradition of Enlightenment after its collapse during the *Third Reich* (i.e. restoration through identity), while Luhmann argued that this was not possible and instead we should look for new ideas that would encompass the complexities of the German experience after their great intellectual and scientific traditions collapsed under imaginable tyranny and collective madness (i.e. restoration through functional difference).

Thus, Luhmann took an uncompromising belief in systems not only as abstract models for society but also as concrete manifestations of society. In borrowing and extrapolating ideas from biology, in particular the ideas of Maturana and Varela (1980) about life as self-producing, self-referential closed systems (autopoiesis) controlled by negative feedback loops (cybernetics), Luhmann embraced the view that society is literally self-organizing autopoietic and cybernetic systems, and therefore systems theory is the only way to understand society.

Habermas throughout his life and career had become 'allergic' to single-minded collective ideology – first in his experience of growing up during the Nazi period, then of Soviet Stalinism, not least in close by Eastern Germany. The problem in totalitarian regimes is the lack of separation between law and morality. Instead, the merging of the two means that contextual truth is replaced by absolute truth. Hence, truth becomes abstract and idealistic.

Luhmann also took an anti-totalitarian view, but his argument was based in systems thinking as a way of enabling difference. Nevertheless, perhaps Habermas saw in Luhmann's radical systems thinking a potential for misuse by fanatic political ideology. One can only recall the story of Bertalanffy (see Chapter 1), who under the Nazi regime easily adapted his holistic systems theory to suit the political purposes of that regime.

In any case, it is clear that Habermas argued for a methodology of reflexive hermeneutic, which not only takes seriously rationality as contextual but also regards the diverse practices emerging from such an attitude as the most important way to protect and uphold the public political discourse of democracy. Luhmann argued that society should be understood as a complex system, which accordingly gains ontological status, meaning that systems are not merely analytical tools but are reality itself. Nevertheless, both Habermas and Luhmann seem to have grappled with how to understand complexity and social reality. While Habermas sought to reconstruct social identity through engaging in political discourse, Luhmann sought to avoid political identity (conformity) through embracing self-organizing social diversity. However, systems thinking lacks an understanding of novelty and emergence of complexity. Such criticism will inevitably go against Luhmann.

Another problem with applying systems thinking as a theory for understanding society is that it potentially eradicates the subject and replaces it with an abstract collective actor, a higher-order faceless body that is given the ability to act (agency) (see Chapter 4). The idea of the collective actor is very close to the holistic systems idea in which higher-order agency is seen in biology (a cell acting as an integrated organism on behalf of itself and differently from its components). If such explanation were to be extrapolated beyond the cell, all biological entities would seem to act according to their own pre-decided way and purpose (teleological), just like Kant proposed, and not according to physical laws under which the subparts of the organism behave. If a purified and radicalized leap of the same idea is made in dealing with the human subject and human society, it would mean that society is a system that acts as a suprasubject according to its own logic and goals, while the individual subject operates according to other premises and causalities. The individual is removed from his or her influence in society, other than to be a detached co-producer of the acting suprasubject. Clearly, if made political, such an idea can only be totalitarian.

Any kind of totalitarian political ideology that came to be experienced during the 20th century is based on the idea of a tyranny of a collective, wherein the superiority of the collective is not only more than but also different from its component parts (human beings). Radical systems thinking is tailor-made to suit such a political purpose, which is why any radicalization of the systems idea is dangerous. This worry seems to underlie Habermas's objections towards Luhmann, even though Luhmann did not suggest anything like totalitarianism – quite the contrary.

Interestingly, Habermas and Luhmann differed with respect to their understanding of complexity although neither of them seemed to pay attention to developments in chaos and complexity theories throughout the period of their debate. Luhmann based his view on 1950s holistic systems theory in combination with autopoiesis, while Habermas pointed to a different basis for understanding complexity in society: the 'forgotten' ideas of philosophical pragmatism and intersubjectivity. As it turned out, Luhmann's systems thinking had a major breakthrough in sociology and it was solidified in organizational theory during the 1980s. Habermas's call for an understanding of society as communicative action, a theory related to Mead's communicative theory (Mead, 1977 [1934]), did not attract nearly as much interest in social theory (Joas and Knöbl, 2009). However, pragmatism attracted new interest in philosophy from the 1980s.

Neo-pragmatism

Renewed philosophical attention towards pragmatism gained momentum as a consequence of the American philosopher Richard Rorty's book *Philosophy and the Mirror of Nature* (Rorty, 1979), in which surprisingly he declared that American pragmatist John Dewey was one of the three most important philosophers of the 20th century, the others being Martin Heidegger and Ludwig Wittgenstein (Joas and Knöbl, 2009, pp. 500–501).

Rorty's book stimulated a debate in philosophy about the importance of pragmatism, not least because the two most important American philosophers in the discussion – Rorty and Hilary Putnam – offered different interpretations of philosophy (Putnam, 1981, 1992, 1995). Putnam critiqued Rorty's view for being inconsistent, particularly with regard to the problem of understanding across cultures. They also differed on the pragmatist view of contextuality.

Rorty interpreted pragmatism as taking a radical stance on contextuality in that, for instance, Wittgenstein's idea of language games – ways of talking and communicating in various cultures – would be secluded and impossible to make sense of across cultures. By contrast, Putnam held that even if a practice such as language, ethics, or a world view were to arise and be understood differently and context-dependent, there would be at the same time a universality to human beings in that their ability to think and communicate, also about what they do not understand, would render them able to communicate across groups and cultures. Such abilities have something to do with the possibility of agreeing on human values to the extent that they can be seen as objective. For Putnam, the key to pragmatism is not context but practice, and it is a failure to think that pragmatism implies completely relative and context-dependent realities, without any enduring or transcending points of reference.

Rorty argued that the pragmatists departed from mainstream philosophy in that they were not dealing with systematic and universal truth (Rorty,

1982). For him, pragmatism meant a form of pure contextuality. Putnam held the view that this was a misinterpretation of the pragmatists, a view supported by Joas and Knöbl (2009, pp. 508–510). They claim: 'Rorty simply ignores crucial topics and achievements of classical pragmatism' (ibid., p. 505).

Rorty's angle towards pragmatism was anchored in political liberalism, where reality begins and ends with the individual. This is reflected in the title of his latest book, *Pragmatism as Anti-Authoritarianism*, edited by Eduardo Mendieta and published posthumously (Rorty, 2021). However, for pragmatists like Mead and Dewey, the very centre of the human condition is the fact that humans are intrinsically (i.e. biologically) social beings. Societies are undoubtedly contextual, but the weakness in Rorty's argument was to think that the reason for this is individuality. However, context can never be individual when the beings involved are social to the core. According to Mead and Dewey, contextuality is always a social phenomenon. Contexts differ because human sociality emerges paradoxically as both general and particular at the same time. The ability to form context is a general and universal human characteristic, but as this generality plays out, differences arise. Therefore, at the centre of Mead's argument was the idea that humans are paradoxical – they construct contextuality and universality at the same time. However, in most social theories, paradox is not easily accepted. Rorty seemed to think that universality cannot exist because everything is contextual, while Putnam seemed to think that everything cannot be contextual because universalities exist. For both philosophers, it seems that a paradox of simultaneous universality and contextuality was problematic.

However, for Mead, the fact that humans produce different social and local contexts does not mean that they have nothing in common. On the contrary, he argued that humans tend to behave in similar ways in similar situations, but in this similarity they also produce small and spontaneous differences that are amplified in the specific context, such that the contextual behaviour, including language, can become very different over time. However, people everywhere still bear the universality of being human, meaning that their ability and wish to communicate; their shifting preferences and affinity to power that can enable them to act while others become constrained; their need to belong to a group or society; and their urge to idealize, value, and create norms of group behaviour are all universal human traits and thus possible to transcend and adapt across multiple groups and societies.

Pragmatists, like Mead, were interested in how humans have evolved as social beings in conjunction with their abilities for communicative action in ever-advanced linguistic symbols and gestures, as well as what it means to become social from the outset (i.e. at birth). Dewey was interested in learning and development processes, and he became a key thinker for researchers of pedagogy and education. Both Dewey and Mead shared and discussed their ideas with each other, and they focused much attention on everyday conflicting and practical experience, somewhat apart from philosophy's enduring theoretical focus on universal principle and truth.

Nevertheless, the clashes between the philosophers Rorty and Putnam over classical pragmatism, which prompted a new interest in this philosophy from the 1980s onwards, were not mirrored in the same energetic way in the social sciences and social theory (Joas and Knöbl (2009, p. 511). The best example of a philosopher who has published consistently on pragmatism, human action, and social practice from the early 1970s is the American pragmatist Richard Bernstein (Bernstein, 1971, 1983, 2010). Another example is Hans Joas, a German social theorist who started his career in 1980 with a thesis on Mead's work, in which he drew attention to Mead's forgotten achievement as a social theorist. Cited in Joas and Knöbl (2009, p. 512), Joas's thesis argued that:

[Mead] had managed to resolve numerous action theoretical problems, at which European social theorists had long slaved away, always in vain, and who also succeeded in producing the first truly viable concept of intersubjectivity through his anthropological theory of communication.

Later, in the 1990s, after including Dewey in his readings, Joas's theory of action was published in his book *The Creativity of Action* (Joas, 1996). In the book he shows that classical sociology had immense difficulties in dealing with human creativity, which in reality has been of crucial importance for the trajectory of human history. Joas's point is not to dichotomize creativity with repetition or routine. His point is that humans are creative in all their actions, even those we term routine (Joas, 1996, p. 514).

At this point, we reach a very important junction as far as complexity theory is concerned. Complexity theory in the natural sciences is really a theory of how something new can arise that has not existed before. As shown in Prigogine's work (see Chapter 4), it is in the spontaneous and unpredictable course of nature brought about by self-organizing processes emerging from interactions and coherent amplification to a critical point (a bifurcation point) that irreversible new order appears and either stabilizes or fluctuates until it collapses. This is the creativity of nature, which in turn produces complexity. In a similar way, human interactions and their ingrained creativity change the courses of organizations and societies.

References

Bernstein, R.J. (1971). *Praxis and Action: Contemporary Philosophies of Human Activity*. Philadelphia, PA: University of Pennsylvania Press.

Bernstein, R.J. (1983). *Beyond Objectivism and Relativism: Science, Hermeneutics, and Praxis*. Philadelphia, PA: University of Pennsylvania Press.

Bernstein, R.J. (2010). *The Pragmatic Turn*. Cambridge, UK: Polity Press.

Bertalanffy, L. von (1950). An outline of a general system theory. *British Journal of Philosophy of Science* 1, pp. 134–165.

Bertalanffy, L. von (1951). General systems theory: A new approach to unity of science. *Human Biology* 23, pp. 303–361.

Bertalanffy, L. von (1968). *General Systems Theory*. New York: George Braziller.

Blumer, H. (1937). Social psychology. In: Schmidt, E.P. (ed.) *Man and Society*, pp. 144–198. New York: Prentice-Hall.

Blumer, H. (1969). *Symbolic Interactionism: Perspectives and Method*. Los Angeles, CA: University of California Press.

Gadamer, H.G. (2013). *Truth and Method*. London: Bloomsbury Academic.

Giddens, A. (1976). *New Rules of Sociological Method*. London: Hutchinson.

Griffin, D. (2002). *The Emergence of Leadership: Linking Self-Organization and Ethics*. London: Routledge.

Habermas, J. (1984). *The Theory of Communicative Action, Volume One: Reason and the Rationalization of Society*. Translated by Thomas A. McCarthy. Boston, MA: Beacon Press.

Habermas, J. (1987). *The Theory of Communicative Action, Volume Two: Lifeworld and System: A Critique of Functionalist Reason*. Translated by Thomas A. McCarthy. Boston, MA: Beacon Press.

Harste, G. (2021). *The Habermas-Luhmann Debate*. New York: Colombia University Press.

Heidegger, M. (1962). *Being and Time*. Oxford: Blackwell.

Hume, D. (1978 [1740]). *A Treatise of Human Nature*. Edited with Analytical Index by L.A. Selby-Bigge. 2nd ed. with text revised and notes by P.H. Nidditch. Oxford: Clarendon Press.

Joas, H. (1996). *The Creativity of Action*. Chicago, IL: University of Chicago Press.

Joas, H. & Knöbl, W. (2009). *Social Theory: Twenty Introductory Lectures*. Cambridge: Cambridge University Press.

Maturana, H.R. & Varela, F.J. (1980). *Autopoiesis and Cognition: The Realization of the Living*. Boston, MA: D. Reidel.

Mead, G.H. (1977 [1934]). *Mind, Self and Society*. Edited and introduced by Charles W. Morris. Chicago, IL: Chicago University Press.

Parsons, T. (1937). *The Structure of Social Action*. New York: McGraw-Hill.

Pavlov, I.P. (1927). *Conditioned Reflexes: An Investigation of the Physiological Activity of the Cerebral Cortex*. Translated by G.V. Anrep. New York: Oxford University Press.

Putnam, H. (1981). *Reason, Truth and History*. Cambridge: Cambridge University Press.

Putnam, H. (1992). *Renewing Philosophy*. Cambridge, MA: Harvard University Press.

Putnam, H. (1995). *Pragmatism: An Open Question*. Oxford: Blackwell.

Rorty, R. (1979). *Philosophy and the Mirror of Nature*. Princeton, NJ: Princeton University Press.

Rorty, R. (1982). *Consequences of Pragmatism*. Minneapolis, MN: University of Minnesota Press.

Rorty, R. (2021). *Pragmatism as Anti-Authoritarianism*. Cambridge, MA: Belknap Press.

Skjervheim, H. (1974a). Objectivism and the study of man (part I). *Inquiry* 17(1–4), pp. 213–239.

Skjervheim, H. (1974b). Objectivism and the study of man (part II). *Inquiry* 17(1–4), pp. 265–302.

Snow, C. & Collini, S. (1993). The Rede lecture (1959): The two cultures. In: Snow, C. (ed.) *The Two Cultures*, pp. 1–52. Cambridge: Cambridge University Press.

Stacey, R.D. (2001). *Complex Responsive Processes in Organizations: Learning and Knowledge Creation*. London: Routledge.

Watson, J.B. (1913). Psychology as a behaviourist views it. *Psychological Review* 20(2), pp. 158–177.

6 Complexity, Philosophy, and Organizational Practice

Complexity and Philosophy

Although there was a development within philosophy and social theory in the 20th century that is helpful as a base for research in organizational theory and complexity, there are two concerns. One is that the relevant theoretical developments in philosophy and social theory do not explicitly address complexity in society and its relation to complexity in nature. There is no coherent philosophy of complexity. The second concern is that the theories and ideas that seem to come close to describing similar complexity phenomena in society to those in nature, and as such hold some potential for being developed in the direction of a social and organizational theory of complexity, have to this day been located in the margins of interest from organizational researchers. Hence, such theory has not received the impetus needed to move to any firm and coherent ground.

Judging from the literature on complexity, philosophy, and social theory, most of the work is anchored in holistic systems theories, which were the first generation of theories attempting to address issues related to complexity. In many cases, attempts to bring new ideas to the discussion are overshadowed by the constant fall back onto traditional systems theories.

In Chapters 3–5, it was discussed how systems theories have tremendous problems at their base, the most notable of which is that they do not take into account the nature of complexity as an integrated process of creation and creativity in nature and society. In this chapter, promising routes towards a coherent complexity theory for organizations is outlined.

Postmodernism and Complexity

One of the most active researchers to explore complexity as a theme in philosophy was Paul Cilliers. He suggested linking complexity to post-structuralism and postmodern philosophy (Cilliers, 1998, 2011), and he

DOI: 10.4324/9781003042501-8

held that complexity theories describe a reality that finds parallels with the thinking of two French philosophers, Jean-Francois Lyotard (Lyotard, 1979) and particularly Jacques Derrida (Cilliers, 2005). Cilliers's reasoning was that if we acknowledge the world as being complex, it implies profound consequences not only for our world view but also for how we can know a complex reality. As the human ability to know and understand complexity is limited, there are always claims about reality that do not bring more clarity to our understanding. This means that our approach must be one of humbleness and ethics in making our claims, a position that does not always match the approach of natural science because there is a conviction that final truths about reality must be discovered, and that humans are capable of discovering these truths. Cilliers complained that there was no modesty in such a position. Moreover, it seemed to him that prestige and politics are involved, because among some natural scientists

> there seems to be a need to dismiss positions that can be called postmodern, post-structural or deconstructive.
>
> (Cilliers, 2005, p. 255)

Nevertheless, Cilliers argued that we need both the natural scientific view towards complexity as well as interpretative knowledge views. In acknowledging the natural science view, Cilliers recognized that models and simplifications are part of human understanding. Hence, even though in favour of *postmodernism*, he did not depart from the systems perspective, which is a profoundly *modernistic* view, but rather defended it, as he called for developing collaboration and bridging between the different ways of thinking:

> Some of the theoretical positions that are being dismissed so assertively, such as deconstruction, help us to cope with these limitations and should not be relegated to the junkyard of history. They should be developed in conjunction with our growing scientific knowledge.
>
> (Cilliers, 2005, p. 256)

Cilliers seemed to be aligned with the traditional position of general systems thinking (see Chapter 1) because the core of this thinking is an argument for gathering multiple and diverse views within a systems frame. Others have argued along the same lines: postmodernism and post-structuralism are the right streams in which to explore complexity (Dillon, 2000; Kuhn and Woog, 2005; Preiser et al., 2013; Woermann et al., 2018). At the same time, these researchers also draw on systems thinking, among others the French systems philosopher Edgar Morin (1992), and thus they keep firmly within the Kantian dual causality view (see Chapter 5). However, Kantian dualism and systems thinking do not explain novelty, creativity, and irreversibility, which are the central themes addressed by the complexity sciences.

Postmodernism encompass a range of ideas that has often been criticized for their lack of clear and objective points of reference. It is fair to say that Cilliers was right in complaining that postmodernist thinkers at times have been misunderstood and subjected to critique based on ignorance. One may also argue that the whole idea of postmodernism is to not have any points of reference because in a complex and perpetually moving world there are no such references to agree on. In this sense, complexity is the key theme that postmodern thought is responding to (Feyerabend, 1975). However, when postmodernist philosophers explicitly mobilize systems thinking to deal with complexity, ideas that seem contradictory in terms, this will inevitably be subjected to the same criticism as the one raised against systems thinking in general (see Chapter 4).

Pragmatism and Complexity

Another possible route to follow is to bring together complexity ideas on time, order, and irreversible process, as reflected in Prigogine's thinking (see Chapter 4), with ideas drawn from philosophical pragmatism and neo-pragmatism, and intersubjective discourse theory (see Chapter 5).

However, one challenge for linking philosophy, social theory, organizational theory, and complexity research is that none of the 20th-century and post–World War II social theorists and philosophers, from whom complexity researchers have drawn on so far, explicitly have explored any such link. However, complexity theories have challenged the dominant views on human organizing (Allen et al., 2011; Johannessen and Kuhn, 2012) and rejected established views based on a fundamental new understanding of the processes of self-organization – in nature, as well as in society. Self-organizing processes are interactional processes by which the activity or action of living entities is structured into organized patterns of behaviour at a more complex scale than that at which the particular organizing is occurring. When we ask how a society can be explained in terms of the interactions between individuals, we are asking how a larger, wider, and more complex scale of organization can be explained in terms of interactions between entities at a less complex scale.

Complexity theories have in common the attention to how the scaling of organization emerges as a result of self-organizing processes rather than as a result of design by someone or something outside the interaction processes. As such patterning processes are self-organizing, they are not linear or predictable. On the contrary, they are non-linear, emergent, and radically unpredictable. Taking this as a point of departure, the challenge of researching organizations and society is to seek understanding of the dynamics of human self-organizing patterning processes and the general human phenomena that are involved in such processes. Hence, complexity theories are concerned with the dynamics of organizing as the detailed, local, self-organizing, and paradoxical processes that are patterning human interactions.

One of the most dramatic implications of complexity research in both the natural and social sciences is the realization that the ideas about effective causality (whereby change is seen as linear movement) and formative causality (whereby change is seen as already embedded in any evolving structure) do not explain movement and change of time, space, history, and organized structures. Instead, changing reality seems to be caused by the self-organizing construction of the movement itself, which is referred to as 'transformative causality' (Prigogine and Stengers, 1984; Stacey, 2001). Irrespective of scale, interaction between entities causes processes, continuity, and change to emerge as structures – physical or social – on a different scale. At the same time, such structures are not reversible and cannot be reduced to their constructing interacting components (Prigogine, 1997; Mainzer, 2009). This is what is meant by structures (organization) *emerging* from self-organizing interactions.

The Emergence of Communicative Actions

In the case of human society, interactions are formed by communicative actions (Habermas, 1984; Bhaktin, 1986). The consequences of such interactions within a short or long time horizon cannot be designed or controlled by anyone because people, in their specific actions, also act spontaneously, and their communication and knowledge are associative (Mead, 1977 [1934]; Bruner, 1990).

The notion of human control of nature and society is a strongly engraved and dominant idea in modern societies. At the same time, human history has shown that at any point in time the future was unpredictable and uncontrollable (Ferguson, 2010). Therefore, the idea of human control of the future is fundamentally dubious. The reality of human interaction (i.e. communication) is that no single person, group, or organization can control how communication moves, let alone control the consequences of communication among myriads of people. Rather, it is the communicational themes that organize human practices and experiences, and these themes of communication are self-organizing, as are any temporal experiences of control. If we accept this description, it is not surprising that different cultures do not become what they become merely because of what their leaders do or the plans they make. When no single person or group can exert control in emergent organizational processes, it is because experiences of control also are experiences of the emergent self-organizing patterns of interaction. Experiences of control can emerge and become present in one moment, only to disappear in the next.

If reality is seen as complex self-organizing processes moving in time and space, then the shifting patterns we call societies are practices that are repeated and changed as ongoing interactions between people in specific groups and contexts. Organizations and societies can neither be designed nor controlled, as they are dynamic patterns of communication emerging in local human interaction (Stacey, 2010).

Communicative patterns are both competitive and collaborative, and they can create harmony as well as conflict. Communicative patterns lead to power dynamics, which regulate and enable behaviours of group inclusion and exclusion (Elias and Scotson, 1994; Dalal, 1998). Thus, organization as practice is strongly dependent on the close self-organizing construction of 'us' identities and 'them' identities.

The Emergence of Identity

In order to understand a group with internal variations, one must look to other groups (Dalal, 1998). This sense of 'other groups', or 'society', has something in common with Mead's idea of 'the generalized other' (Mead, 1977 [1934]). Experiences of the generalized other influence and regulate how a group becomes cohesive. They also contribute to a group's tendency to perform similar actions in similar contexts. Most people behave in similar ways in public, despite not knowing each other or having spoken together, or in any way having agreed on how to behave. Mead's understanding of the phenomenon is that it happens because each person imagines, observes, and generalizes what others do. In this way, public social behaviour is regulated, coordinated, and organized. Moreover, both individual and group identities are created as different aspects of these ongoing social interaction processes.

Consider the development of language and thinking. Humans develop linguistic abilities while becoming functional human beings. Every person develops an identity, which is both individual and social at the same time. At any point in a person's development, it will be difficult to use the expression 'I am' without referring to 'we are' and vice versa. Humans are not constructing processes of social identity outside their interacting bodies (Burkitt, 1999). Identity is an emerging and simultaneous process of mind, self, and society (Mead, 1977 [1934]). In this sense, communication is the basis of organizing identity and belonging in time and space (Shotter, 1993).

Thus, understanding the patterning properties of human communication is to understand the processes by which humans stand out as individuals, at the same time as they create small and large group identities. Who or what is organizing such patterning processes? Complexity theory implies that the patterning processes are self-organizing and emerging, meaning that the dynamic patterning creates complexity at different scales at the same time and without any central actor or powerful designer. There is no first and second with individuals and society. One does not come before the other, and there is no mutual construction. They both emerge at the same time as two aspects of the same transformative process.

The Emergence of Coordination

Performing a social practice means *anticipating* how others will tend to act in different situations (Blumer, 1969). At the same time, the detailed individual actions will vary from situation to situation, such that the organized patterns are never repeated exactly in the same way. Even though patterns are mostly recognizable, they are also dynamic and cannot be predicted when seen from the perspective of the individual actor. Such simultaneous generalized and flexible patterns of action, which include the use of physical objects and natural environments, were termed *social objects* by Mead (1912). A social object is not the same as a physical object, although it includes how physical objects enter into human action (Johannessen and Stacey, 2005). A social object is a simultaneously generalized and particularized pattern of behaviour. *Generalized patterns* are a behaviour that is recognized as typical of a group or wider society. *Particularized patterns* are endless variations and specificities in the actions and ways of thinking of individuals.

Patterns that are specific to a person make it possible to separate with precision specific actions at specific places at specific times. However, this specificity tends to disappear when people refer to a generalized practice in a group, organization, or society. From an individual's perspective, human action, interactional processes, and groups tend to become so diffuse that they are simplified as static objects and confounded with physical objects and systems. What is specific in human practice is then reified and made into a static object, as if it were a physical object. Thus, objectified reductions (i.e. physical objects) and static distance are constructed of what are (and have been) complex intersubjective and interactional processes in time-space (i.e. social objects). Therefore, descriptions of detailed, real organizational practices are often replaced with abstract, simplified, and generalized categories of behaviour. However, it is not the abstract physical object or system that is coordinated action, it is the social object.

The Emergence of Moral and Ethics

The various ways of communication and power relations are deeply anchored in experiences of identity, and the purpose of what one is doing. Additionally, people who are dependent on the practices they perform make different judgements and evaluations of other people in relation to themselves and their group. In other words, they enact different notions of moral and ethics, what is right and what is necessary to do, and what it means to perform good acts in different contexts. As the paradoxical patterns of identity emerge, so too do the notions of right and wrong, good and bad, and the value of other people, which are moral and ethical ideas.

Joas (2000) holds that human morality is the notions and experiences of what one must or should do or be (i.e. obligations and norms). Morality constrains human behaviour. By contrast, ethics are the notions and experiences of what one hopes to do or be (i.e. ideals and values). Such ideals and values enable human behaviour. Conflicts between moral constraints and ethical emancipation are experienced as paradoxical tensions in human existence. Ethics and values are free of conflict because they are idealizations of reality. For example, we can all agree that freedom and justice is good (ethical). However, we often disagree on what freedom and justice means for a particular individual in everyday practical terms (moral). Moral is always a source of practical conflict. Hence, moral-ethical thinking is both enabling and constraining and as such it coincides with the phenomena of power, violence, and authority.

The Emergence of Power, Violence, and Authority

Humans cannot exist without power and they cannot escape from power. As underlined by Elias (2000), power does not belong to any individual; it is a social phenomenon. In contrast to *violence*, which is the direct and instrumental application of force by someone or something with immediate effect on one or more persons, power is the potential for action and regulation that can only rise or flow from a community (i.e. a group or organized pattern of behaviour). In this sense, power is related to authority.

Thus, power is generally organized, whereas violence is not (Arendt, 1970; Foucault, 2003). Violence is purely an instrumental gesture towards the immediate future; it is meant to disrupt and create chaos in an already existing organized power pattern, which in turn has come about because of a certain repetition of behaviour during a period of time. As pointed out by Hannah Arendt in her analysis of the Holocaust, the fusion of power and violence into organized violence is particularly destructive or eradicating because it does not stop, even if those who perform the violence have full control over existing power relations. Enforced in a society, violence then becomes *totalitarian* (Arendt, 1951), a human condition that in no way is sustainable because stable social government can only emerge out of power figurations and the self-organizing restraining of violent behaviour – e.g. self-discipline in group behaviour (Elias, 2000; Foucault, 2003). However, such a phase change from totalitarian violence towards restraining of violent behaviour depends on self-inflicted calm, order, and even apathy under authoritarian repressive rule. It is a condition that the Czech writer and political dissident Vaclav Havel termed *post-totalitarian* (Havel, 1992, p. 131) in an essay originally written in 1978 describing the chilling atmosphere that had engulfed society in the wake of the Soviet communist bloc military invasion of Czechoslovakia in 1968.

Nevertheless, the dynamics of organized structuring has always been radically unpredictable. Individual variation and sudden fluctuations in a specific practice can sometimes amplify and lead to significant organizational crises and collapse of organized patterns within a short period (Diamond, 2005). The whole bloc of eastern European communist regimes collapsed during a few months in 1989, and in 1991 the extremely militarized one-party state and superpower Soviet Union disintegrated from within. One implication of this experience is that organizations never become what they become because of a hierarchy (Johannessen, 2018). In everyday reality, responsibility and influence do not flow clearly through a power hierarchy. When organizations and societies emerge as a result of what many people do in their different interactional practises, and when those processes are formed by experiences of communication, power relations, identity, norms, and values, there are no simple connections between hierarchical position and how organizations evolve.

As power figurations emerge, so too does the experience of *authority* as a particular quality of the power figuration. Authority was already in Roman times closely linked to organizing: the Roman term *auctoritas* was used to denote the power that was flowing from either the Senate or the Emperor. Thus, the word *author*, having the same etymological origin, can be understood as a person (the authority) who writes the rules, as someone who commands the language and the themes of communication, which in complexity terms is the same as 'one who organizes'. The author or authority symbolizes a particular distance in the power figuration, meant to invoke submission, idealization, and glorification. Performing this distance with clarity, as the *authoritarian*, is the same as the organization controlling the boundaries of violent behaviour, a behaviour just within the limits of constraining violence, while at the same time being willing, if necessary, to apply the dominant means of violence. This is exactly what authorities do in a modern state; they control the legitimate use of violence (in terms of the police and the military).

Regulating the level of chaos (violent behaviour) is a necessary condition for the establishment of a geographical area associated with a state. Such behaviour demands the crossing of the boundary between patterns of violent chaos and authoritarian rule as a stabilizing power constellation (Arendt, 1970; Agamben, 2005). The emergence of organization must include this stabilizing of power figurations at the same time as the dynamics of free activity moves and changes short-term patterns. Using the language of chaos theory (Gleick, 1987), we could say that the way organizations are held together by authority and power constellations is the analogue of a strange attractor, around which chaos rotates and patterns constantly shift.

A Note on Time and Organizational Practice

We can interpret the emergence of organizing by understanding that humans are fundamentally communicative, and that their social identity, power relations, and moral ethics emerge in human communicative practice. In this sense, communicative practice is a continuous *practice of organization*. It follows that organizing can neither be linear nor be planned, as communication does not follow the logic of linearity and planning. How, then, can a society seem organized, and activity seemingly be planned and implemented by people in powerful positions?

Being organized can only be seen in hindsight. Future reality is always *disorganized* because it is self-organizing, non-linear, and emerging. The past is always *organized* because we have structured it, made sense of it, and made it linear (which in complexity terms is not real). A great part of our communicative practice is directed towards creating meaning in the world, by which we *organize our past experiences*.

It is in the organization of past experience that we *organize reality* (history), an activity that might be confused with *reality being organized* for us by 'someone', such as a powerful leader. When reality is being organized in this way, it means that we adhere to and find meaning in a fantasy about the future, which powerful leader figures formulate in the form of visions that make people feel part of an enlarged group identity with unrealistic ideas of what the group can achieve. People act on the basis of such fantasies. However, reality is constructed as people act and therefore acting with intention on the basis of a particular objective, which is formed individually or in a group, will have an impact on how reality is constructed. Because people's actions always create stretched out time horizons – actions simultaneously creating past, present, and future – any actor might experience structure integrated into their actions on the basis of fantasies. As this happens, reality seems organized in the present, while it is only past experiences that are organized. The future is still open.

Thus, to claim that someone has implemented a plan is also to imply that all disturbances, discussions, compromises, persuasions, threats, briberies, flattering, and luring, have been neglected in the process. Such disturbances are the reasons why a plan never ends up being implemented in the way powerful people intended it to be. Even if implementing a plan is a form of power play that some master better than others, there are always many people involved. If we investigate the details of organizational processes, we will find that they are always messy. How people behave, communicate, and understand what actions they should perform at any moment, as well as how they understand the actions they have already performed, is never part of an overall plan, as all actions are also *inter*actions that are meant for, and will have consequences in, the non-organized future, whereas a plan is an organized version of the future – a hope that something will happen in the future that can turn out to become the organized past.

Thus, a plan is a *hope* for a *future organized past* rather than a prediction or intention of practice in *the reality of the future*. As such, a plan is an attempt at an *ethical* gesture, an idealistic notion free of human conflict, meant to inspire and gather a group for coordinated action, only to be sharpened and changed into real action in reality's conflicting practices. The result is often something *different* from the plan and the outcome is unpredictable. This is what society and humans evolving in self-organizing processes mean.

We see the organized past either as human's general organizing abilities or as qualities for actions pointing to the future. These human abilities and qualities are communication, identity, power, and moral ethics, and they organize people through experiences of meaning (i.e. structures of individual and group actions). They also organize explanations of why things became the way they became (and become the way they become).

Short-term and Long-term Cultures

In the emergence of organization, we can differentiate between *short-term culture* and *long-term culture*. Short-term culture is the immediate and everyday chaotic future being organized by the actors. This is highly dynamic and receptive to spontaneity, creativity, and change. Long-term culture is held in place by enduring values rooted in the conscious and unconscious social patterns of a group or society of people. It is linked to repetition of tradition, rituals, and social habits. It is a way of behaving and thinking in time and space where people take for granted their acceptance and valuation of a certain way of being. The values are internalized and anchored as basic assumptions about what it means to be human in that particular society – generation after generation. It is a long-term *identity rhythm*. Values such as freedom, justice, and equality do not get into people's psyche as immediate or temporal phenomena. Values are created and re-created in a society over long periods of time until their meanings are taken for granted (Joas, 2000).

The way in which values are practised expresses a long-term culture, even if the practising of the values in everyday situations can change and bring new short-term cultural expressions. Throughout long periods of time, short-term changes are amplified, sharpened, or removed by the changes and compromises of everyday problems and conflicts. Long-term compromises and solutions are spun out from the short-term culture's pragmatic, spontaneous, and elastic chaos.

Organization is a space-time where the messy short-term culture is starting to whirl around in perpetual change and movement, while at the same time a long-term culture is being created and re-created as stabilizing, though moveable, reference points. Thus, organization is the analogue of the strange attractor in chaos theory. In a certain time and space it can be experienced and even observed, but nevertheless not defined, pinned down, or predicted. It is a space–time area where a resilient and widespread identity rhythm (long-term culture) establishes itself sufficiently to resist the continuous impulses of collapse and fragmentation brought about by the immediate short-term culture, and at the same time it is transparent enough to exploit and organize the energy impulses provided by the chaos, so that a holding pattern is created, a pattern in which change, adaptation, resource attraction, growth, expansion, and diversification of groups is sustained.

Time Horizons, Rhythm, and Reality

In the different organizing practices, we can imagine a differentiation based on *organized identity rhythms* – chronological rhythms, individual rhythms, social rhythms, work rhythms, rhythms in relation to nature and animals, and religious and/or spiritual rhythms. The rhythms define experiences of time subjectively (individual time) and socially (social time). Elasticity in rhythm and time experiences is a human capacity and defines how we can change tempo in our activities and thought patterns. The human brain has been shown to possess the ability for both fast and slow thinking (Kahnemann, 2011), which implies the ability for fast and slow decision-making. This means that the human brain possesses time elasticity, which is an asset for changing rhythms of living. At the same time, there are individual differences and limits to this ability.

Groups or organized rhythms are patterns of our participation that we become accustomed to, rhythms that we thrive on while enacting. Our individual rhythm is a baseline or reference point for a time horizon in which we gaze forwards and backwards in real present time. From this 'multi-' time-space view, in which reality is seen as in perpetual movement in the present, we organize the past and look towards the chaotic and unknown future in search for objective reference points that can function as guidance for our immediate or strategic actions in the unknown waters of the future, like flashes from a lighthouse. The horizon we gaze at behind us and in front of us is our *individual and social time horizon*. Even if we as humans know that the future reality is totally unknown, we nevertheless seem to imagine objective reality in the future. The rhythm, in which the time horizon is created and re-created, represents the limit of our imagination of action. The limit to how flexible we can be in relation to other individuals, groups, activities, and other forms of rhythms is constrained by the elasticity of our practices' rhythms. Each and every one of us, now and in the past, cannot be or cannot have been in just any rhythm or group. We are attracted to a group that fits with our own preferred rhythm and the kind of variation allowed by both our own sense of rhythm and that of the group or organization.

The Importance of Crisis for Complexity

Societies can be described as self-organizing patterning processes. Complexity theories explain a type of dynamics that is neither stability nor chaos, but a dynamism that creates complexity at different scales at the same time, as a result of interactions. These processes are accelerated by crises. Thus, crisis and complexity are closely connected as drivers of the movement of time-space by discontinuous reorganizing of reality. Crises (non-equilibrium) expand normal rhythms and movements of time and space, in the creation of complexity. In natural evolution, life emerged as a result of crisis (Kauffmann, 1993; Gell-Mann, 1994; Prigogine, 1997; Holland, 1995). Throughout human history, crises and wars have been major enablers of change in societies (Foucault, 2003; Diamond, 2005; Ferguson, 2010). To define and link the dynamics of crises to time-space complexity dynamics implies to investigate how processes of structuration evolve, including how social structures (i.e. organizations) emerge.

When dealing in the present with knowledge of time-space reality, it is often assumed (or tempting to think) that time-space is reversible and symmetrical. However, complexity theory implies that current time-space necessarily interferes with irreversible and asymmetrical time-space (which is the experience of the movement of real time-space), and it creates a new abstracted and reified version of time-space re-created as the past. Thus, perspectives on time, space, and movement of history are methodologically important in organizational complexity studies.

References

Agamben, G. (2005). *State of Exception*. Chicago, IL: University of Chicago Press.
Allen, P., Maguire, S. & McKelvey, B. (eds.) (2011). *The SAGE Handbook of Complexity and Management*. London: SAGE.
Arendt, H. (1951). *The Origins of Totalitarianism*. Orlando, FL: Harcourt.
Arendt, H. (1970). *On Violence*. New York: Harcourt.
Bhaktin, M.M. (1986). *Speech Genres and Other Late Essays*. Austin, TX: University of Texas Press.
Blumer, H. (1969). *Symbolic Interactionism: Perspectives and Method*. Los Angeles, CA: University of California Press.
Bruner, J. (1990). *Acts of Meaning*. Cambridge, MA: Harvard University Press.
Burkitt, I. (1999). *Bodies of Thought: Embodiment, Identity and Modernity*. London: SAGE.
Cilliers, P. (1998). *Complexity and Postmodernism: Understanding Complex Systems*. London: Routledge.
Cilliers, P. (2005). Complexity, deconstruction and relativism. *Theory, Culture & Society* 22(5), pp. 255–267.
Cilliers, P. (2011). Complexity, poststructuralism and organisation. In: Allen, P., Maguire, S. & McKelvey, B. (eds.) *The SAGE Handbook of Complexity and Management*, pp. 142–154. London: SAGE.
Dalal, F. (1998). *Taking the Group Seriously: Towards a Post-Foulkesian Group Analytic Theory*. London: Jessica Kingsley.
Diamond, J. (2005). *Collapse: How Societies Choose to Fail or Survive*. New York: Penguin.
Dillon, M. (2000). Poststructuralism, complexity and poetics. *Theory, Culture & Society* 17(1), pp. 1–26.
Elias, N. (2000). *The Civilizing Process: Sociogenetic and Psychogenetic Investigations*. Revised ed. Oxford: Blackwell.
Elias, N. & Scotson, J.L. (1994). *The Established and the Outsiders: A Sociological Enquiry into Community Problems*. London: SAGE.
Ferguson, N. (2010). Complexity and collapse: Empires on the edge of chaos. *Foreign Affairs* March/April, pp. 18–32.
Feyerabend, P.K. (1975). *Against Method: Outline of an Anarchistic Theory of Knowledge*. London: New Left Books.
Foucault, M. (2003). *Society Must Be Defended: Lectures at the Collège de France, 1975–76*. New York: Picador.
Gell-Mann, M. (1994). *The Quark and the Jaguar: Adventures in the Simple and the Complex*. New York: W.H. Freeman.
Gleick, J. (1987). *Chaos: Making of a New Science*. New York: Viking Penguin.
Habermas, J. (1984). *The Theory of Communicative Action, Volume One: Reason and the Rationalization of Society*. Translated by Thomas A. McCarthy. Boston, MA: Beacon Press.

Havel, V. (1992). *Open Letters. Selected Writings 1965–1990.* New York, NY: Vintage Books.

Holland, J.H. (1995). *Hidden Order.* Reading, MA: Addison-Wesley.

Joas, H. (2000). *The Genesis of Values.* Cambridge: Polity Press.

Johannessen, S.O. (2018). *Strategies, Leadership and Complexity in Crisis and Emergency Operations.* New York: Routledge.

Johannessen, S.O. & Kuhn, L. (2012). *Complexity in Organization Studies.* Four-volume set (One, Two, Three, and Four). London: SAGE.

Johannessen, S.O. & Stacey, R.D. (2005). Technology as social object: A complex responsive processes perspective. In: Stacey, R.D. (ed.) *Experiencing Emergence in Organisations: Local Interaction and the Emergence of Global Patterns,* pp. 142–163. London: Routledge.

Kahnemann, D. (2011). *Thinking Fast and Slow.* New York: Farrar, Straus, and Giroux.

Kauffmann, S.A. (1993). *The Origins of Order: Self-Organization and Selection in Evolution.* Oxford: Oxford University Press.

Kuhn, L. & Woog, R. (2005). Vortical postmodern ethnography: Introducing a complexity approach to systemic social theorizing. *Systems Research and Behavioral Science* 22, pp. 139–150.

Lyotard, J.-F. (1979). *The Postmodern Condition: A Report on Knowledge.* Minneapolis, MI: Minnesota University Press.

Mainzer, K. (2009). Challenges of complexity in the 21st century: An interdisciplinary introduction. *European Review* 17(2), pp. 219–236.

Mead, G.H. (1912). The Mechanism of Social Consciousness. *The Journal of Philosophy, Psychology and Scientific Methods* 9(15), pp. 401–406.

Mead, G.H. (1977 [1934]). *Mind, Self and Society.* Edited and introduced by Charles W. Morris. Chicago: Chicago University Press.

Morin, E. (1992). From the concept of system to the paradigm of complexity. *Journal of the Social and Evolutionary Systems* 15(4), pp. 371–385.

Preiser, R., Cilliers, P. & Human, O. (2013). Deconstruction and complexity: A critical economy. *South African Journal of Philosophy* 32(3), pp. 261–273.

Prigogine, I. (1997). *The End of Certainty: Time, Chaos and the New Laws of Nature.* New York: The Free Press.

Prigogine, I. & Stengers, I. (1984). *Order Out of Chaos: Man's New Dialogue with Nature.* New York: Bantam Books.

Shotter, J. (1993). *Conversational Realities: Constructing Life Through Language.* Thousand Oaks, CA: SAGE.

Stacey, R.D. (2001). *Complex Responsive Processes in Organizations: Learning and Knowledge Creation.* London: Routledge.

Stacey, R.D. (2010). *Complexity and Organizational Reality: Uncertainty and the Need to Rethink Management after the Collapse of Investment Capitalism.* London: Routledge.

Woermann, M., Human, O. & Preiser, R. (2018). General complexity: A philosophical and critical perspective. *Emergence: Complexity and Organization* 20(2). doi: 10.emerg/10.17357.c9734094d98458109d25b79d546318af

7 Complexity Ideas in Strategy and Organizational Dynamics

Implications and Applications for Organizational Practice

During the three decades that have passed since the time when complexity theories were first introduced in organizational studies, publications on central themes in organizations have broadly fallen into four categories. Those in the first category describe phenomena from chaos and complexity research in the natural sciences, and then argue that qualitative insights are important for *understanding* how organizations and societies evolve (e.g. Stacey, 1995; Campbell-Hunt, 2007; Ferguson, 2010). Publications in the second category argue that the insights from chaos and complexity research in the natural sciences imply a *changed way of talking* about organizations by using a metaphorical language (e.g. Chettiparamb, 2006; Hodge and Coronado, 2007). Those in the third category critique established organizational theories because such theories *fail to explain* the realities and phenomena of complexity in organizations (e.g. Maguire and McKelvey, 1999; Zhu, 2007; Arthur, 2014). Publications in the fourth category refer to the findings of complexity in the natural sciences in order to *apply* those ideas in the creation of new and specific suggestions or solutions to how to perform organizational work and management (e.g. Levinthal, 1997; Anderson, 1999; McKelvey, 1999; MacIntosh and MacLean, 1999, 2001; McGuiness and Morgan, 2000; Cunha and Cunha, 2006; Eisenhardt and Piezunka, 2011). Publications in the first three categories focus on implication, whereas those in the fourth focus on application.

Whereas the *implications* of complexity thinking potentially are the consequences of priorities of attention, *applications* are work and experimentation with new ideas in practice, and the provision of normative advice about what leaders and organizational actors ought to be doing in order to achieve better results. Thus, implications are associated with describing, observing, reflecting, exploring, and suggesting, whereas applications are

DOI: 10.4324/9781003042501-9

associated with prescribing, intervening, and evaluating results. It could also be said that implications are related to understanding, whereas applications are related to practical solutions. In this chapter, research on implications and applications of complexity ideas in strategy and organizational dynamics is presented and discussed.

Strategy and Change

Strategy, together with leadership and management, was one of the first themes explored in the new complexity literature on organizations from the early 1990s. Ralph D. Stacey, one of the pioneering and innovative thinkers of complexity in organizational studies, suggested that the complexity sciences offer new insights into change processes, and hence to ways of understanding strategy in organizations, in contrast to the basic assumptions of two dominant ways of thinking about strategy processes (Stacey, 1995). The two perspectives are the *strategic choice perspective*, which sees powerful leaders as choosing the future direction on behalf of the organizations under their responsibility, and the *evolutionary perspective*, in which organizations are perceived to survive because they are selected through competition in a market. Stacey argued that in both cases equilibrium is assumed, thus not allowing for any proper theory of how strategies and emerging novelty come about.

By contrast, the complexity sciences offer a radically different view and suggest that leaders and other organizational actors should recognize that when they are making plans and acting intentionally, the future is unknown to them and everyone else. Stacey argued that this clearly must lead to consequences for the activity of strategy-making and strategy research.

McGuiness and Morgan (2000) presented a similar critique when they contrasted insights from the complexity sciences with the resource-based strategy view (Penrose, 1959; Prahalad and Hamel, 1990), in which a firm's competitive advantage is determined by its access to human, natural, and technological resources. The resource-based view is based on similar assumptions about the nature of change to those of the above-mentioned evolutionary perspective, in that it assumes that organizations compete as organisms with their available resources and that those best adapted will sustain and grow. Interestingly, an important idea of the resource-based view is that the competitive resources are based on novelty (i.e. innovation) created by people and their knowledge and skills, as well as on money, time for research, and the creation of markets new to the world (Nonaka and Takeuchi, 1995). At the same time, the resource-based view turns to historical data to inform the present and the future and offers no explanation of how novelty comes about.

McGuiness and Morgan (2000) criticize the conflict between relying on innovative capabilities for achieving competitive advantage, while at the same time seeing them as manageable and controllable. Instead, they argue for the usefulness of ideas and analogies from the complexity sciences. They propose that the notion of emergent processes of strategic change is more helpful in determining the roles that executives can and cannot play in forming strategy in a changing world.

An early metaphorical description of complexity was the term 'the edge of chaos' (Lewin, 1992). Cunha and Cunha (2006) and Brown and Eisenhardt (1998) reconceptualized strategy as the art of maintaining the organization at the edge of chaos, a space where freedom and direction allegedly combine to produce creative outputs. Similarly, Carlisle and McMillan (2006) argued that organizations would need to 'dance' between 'the edge of chaos' and 'the edge of stability' if they were to create a sustainable advantage. Maguire and McKelvey (1999) acknowledged that metaphorical applications of complexity science were generating insights, but they cautioned that metaphors needed to be deployed explicitly as such, rather than unreflexively accepted as valid alternative organizational ontologies.

In another use of the language from the complexity sciences, Campbell-Hunt (2007) suggested that organizations and strategies be seen as complex adaptive systems that carry important implications for the scope of practitioners' agency in leading strategic change and for the design of research strategies to investigate complex phenomena. Boje (2000) concluded that change and strategy are self-organizing processes. The complexity of these processes makes the organization sensitive to non-linearity, where small changes can escalate rapidly and potentially bring the organization down.

Eisenhardt and Piezunka (2011) contrasted traditional corporate strategy with a multiple business unit organization, seen as a complex adaptive systems consisting of modular, loosely linked, and unique business units that collaborate and compete with one another. The latter perspective is business unit-centric; it focuses on processes such as 'morphing', 'rewiring', and 'patching'. It also generates quite different prescriptions than traditional theories of the distribution of power and decision-making in firms, the roles of actors, and the management of change. The complexity perspective emphasized in the article by Eisenhardt and Piezunka underlines the importance of a moderate degree of structure and the pursuit of co-evolutionary adaptation of multiple business-unit organizations with their dynamic organizational environments.

Organizational Dynamics

As organizations have grown increasingly global, virtual, and less locally distinct, any general and ideal normative advice about what leaders should be doing has created a restricted space for local action. Even though prescriptions might seem to provide more clarification than merely describing or reflecting upon a situation, what is often skipped in popular management books that provide advice on what leaders should be doing is that normative statements have to be interpreted through local interaction, a process that inevitably leads to locally specific outcomes. Who leaders want to engage with and what they want to say and do in their everyday work are just as much a local cultural issue as a matter of what kinds of general management tools and advice are available (Stacey, 2007).

Complexity researchers share the basic view that strategies and organized patterns of action are *emerging* processes (Stacey, 1995; Lissack, 1999; Black and Farias, 2000; Goldstein, 2000). Such processes evolve in new and unexpected ways through interactions taking place in self-organizing and dynamic ways between actors, which could be individuals, groups, organizations, or societies, in integration and interaction with natural and technological environments (Arthur, 1989; Allen, 1998; Streatfield, 2001; Johannessen and Stacey, 2005). Complexity perspectives depict a world of uncertainty and contingency, in which attempts at control, choice, and predictions of the future are viewed as highly limited and often futile. Nevertheless, it is also a paradoxical world, which in the case of the influence of individual action would mean that an individual both can and cannot influence the trajectory of the future. Organizations evolve and become what they become because people do something all the time. However, to do something with or without intention will both turn out and not turn out as intended. In many, perhaps most, ordinary situations, people manage to do what they set out to do or what they have constructed a routine for doing.

Thus, in many everyday situations, things will turn out broadly as planned for an enormous number of people around the world, mainly because people act in ways that *enable other people* to do what they planned without knowing their plans. Organizations and societies are vast coordination patterns where no one directs the patterns, but everyone contributes to them. This is even more astonishing than the fact that things do not turn out according to plan. Considering how much people discuss and disagree about just about everything in organizations and societies, the most interesting question to ask is perhaps how unplanned coordination of plans can happen.

Strategy Plans

People most often engage in actions in a way that make sense to them (Weick, 1995). Hence, there is an ingrained flawed logic to think that making plans is the same as getting things done. Rather, it is quite the reverse: everyone is dependent on not following their own specific plan, and on others to not follow their specific plans, in order to get things done (Elias, 2000).

Strategy plans are often made of a group of top leaders on behalf of an organization that might include thousands of people's daily actions. The plans might make sense to the leaders, but the shape of a strategy plan is often very general and abstract, describing how the organization must take seriously the market situations or the public situation and from there develop new ideas. However, the actual practice in which such statements are made real will vary greatly and be manifested in all kinds of ways, primarily because many people have to make sense of what it means in their particular practice, and secondarily because all the people in the organization interact with a lot of other organizations and people in their supply chains or networks (Nilsson, 2019). The top executives of the other organizations have constructed their own strategy plans, which again are different from each other's plans. These strategy plans must also make sense to the employees in those organizations.

Ultimately, a given organization will be entangled in so many twists and turns in their practices that a particular strategy plan, which is meant to plan the future, will rarely become the real future. In taking a complexity view of organizations, it is clear that this ought to have consequences for how strategic planning is understood and conducted (Sanders, 1998; Byrne, 2003). However, the paradox is that it is likely that most leaders and managers in organizations will know that the activity of strategy planning is a waste of time, but they will carry out the activity with other purposes in mind than what is claimed rhetorically.

Strategy plans might be expected from investors or authorities in the case of public organizations. Furthermore, the plans might be a way for management groups to do something seemingly meaningful together. Planning the future of an organization is a practice associated with a sense of power that the involved members can hold as a group, in contrast to others in the organization. Alternatively, strategy plans could be a way for leaders to assess the competence of other leaders in the senior management group; the planning process could be a crucial part of the power game at the top level of the hierarchy, whereby rhetoric; communication skills; and the ability to persuade, convince, and attract support from other leaders are tested. Such processes are important for the 'game of thrones', in which leaders close to the top level of the organizational hierarchy position themselves for promotion, power, and influence.

Because organizations are not just simple and strict routine practice but also expressions of how many people interact with colleagues, competitors, clients, and suppliers, the emerging results will be influenced by the dynamics of interactions between all of those people's attempts to shape the next step of their personal future. This means that ordinary everyday life in organizations is not predictable when it comes to the specific activity and results of the organization, even though many tasks are performed routinely and according to expectations.

It is noteworthy that, despite the belief in planning, the term *exceeding expectations* is very popular among leaders because it means they have succeeded even more in the competition than they had planned. Although the term is meant to be motivating and positive, it also means that things did not go according to what was planned. This implies that leaders in one sense do *not* want the organization to evolve according to plan. However, they only want the result to deviate in a positive way, and in such cases they rarely ask why the results turned out the way they did, other than to allocate them to heroic stories of great leadership or great performance. In the opposite case, blame stories are produced about bad leadership and bad performance (Taylor, 2005). It seems inconceivable that the results will have anything to do with an emerging pattern of unplanned coordination of plans without any reversible causation that can be traced back either to heroic individuals or to individuals with a lack of character and morale.

In many of today's organizations, employees and leaders are involved in many more interactions than was the case in earlier working organizations. People in organizations are privately and professionally bombarded with information and interactions through various communication platforms. In complexity terms, interactions are the crucial driving force for change and dynamics. Therefore, our day and age invites an immense level of complexity, which means that all phenomena associated with complexity, such as self-organization, emergence, paradox, non-linearity, and non-equilibrium, are integrated experiences in people's lives. Complexity does not come from outside anything. Human lives are and have always been synonymous with complexity, but the level of interaction and complexity has increased. The number of people on the planet has more than doubled in the past 50 years and has increased by more than 5 billion since 1950, when modern organizational theory in the form of systems theory was born. Since the 1990s, many boundaries that were created earlier in history between countries and people have vaporized. Therefore, to reframe earlier views on organizations in order to take seriously the nature and consequences of complexity is not a marginal issue – it is at the centre of all organizational actors' experiences.

The Problem of Coordination

Traditional organizational theories (Taylor, 1911; Fayol, 1949 [1919]) insisted that organizations needed to be organized in pyramid-shaped hierarchies or at least in some type of controlled structure. Accordingly, leaders should be tasked with managing the organization from a central position at the top of the pyramid or from an imagined position either at the centre of or outside the structure. The idea is that this would create a best possible situational awareness for those inhabiting the most powerful point in the structure, based on all information available from the organizational activity. Decisions should then be based on this understanding, which is termed strategic, and after they have been made they should be communicated to all actors in the organization in order to create a best possible shared understanding of the situations from which the decisions have flowed. After the actors have received the decisions, they should coordinate themselves in their respective departments and groups in such a way that the end result becomes coherent and compliant with the way the strategic decision makers have assumed and predicted. Although slightly simplified, this way of thinking about organizations and leadership is nevertheless widespread. It is a consequence of the idea that organizations are systems that can be coordinated, directed, and managed by leaders.

However, the notion assumes that organizations have linear power structures and that they have stable working processes, as in a state of equilibrium. Complexity theory shows that this assumption is false. A 'large organization' has different areas (groups) that are relatively independent of each other in its functioning. The fact that functions and tasks are carried out in similar ways in different areas enables coordination without hierarchies. As an example, the standardization of working processes makes fast food restaurants, as well as hotels and car manufacturers, operate in similar ways in many different places. However, this coordination does not seem to happen in a hierarchical way, but rather as parallel activities and between distributed structures across the organizations (Axelrod, 1997, 2006). Persons in one area might interact directly with persons in other areas without going through the central point or a leader of all the activities. Most of those interactions would overlap with each other. Such myriad interactions could be very tight and complex, but hardly random. On the contrary, such interactions are highly structured and they function in what could be called coupled local networks.

In such dynamic architectures, people construct and interpret information. It is on the basis of this activity that we can talk about a coordination of understanding, even if the understanding is not common to all; it is the *self-organizing of different understandings* (Johannessen, 2018). There is a big difference between the operational logic in complex dynamic structures and the one in linear hierarchical structures. Human organizations function the way they do because they are complex and not because they are linear. This is because human beings interact and communicate as social actors in very advanced ways. To understand how coordinated patterns of action emerge on the basis of non-hierarchical structures and distributed functions is of central importance to complexity research on organizations.

Crisis, Security, and Strategy

The historian Niall Ferguson uses the metaphor of *edge of chaos* to describe the dynamics of large-scale organized activity (Ferguson, 2010). In assessing the dynamics of political empires throughout time from a complexity perspective he argues that empires in the past have expanded to massive proportions, stabilized for an unknown period of time, and then abruptly collapsed. Hence, growth and collapse of large-scale organizations happens in a non-linear fashion. This leads Ferguson to warn that also present-day large-scale organizations and political 'empires', such as the United States and the European Union, might change very quickly and apparently without any predictable and rational cause.

In a related thematic track, interest has grown to apply complexity thinking in researching crises, security and emergency organizations (Johannessen, 2018). Raisio et al. (2020) explored Finnish military officers' views and perceptions on complexity and found that although the officers were aware that complexity was ingrained in their professional area, complexity ideas could be a useful way of making sense of the security environment. In this context, using complexity ideas to understand how organizational strategies evolve and influence organizational dynamics during crisis and emergency operations is an important theme for research.

In two cases of crisis and emergency operations in Norway involving the Royal Norwegian Air Force and the Police, the detailed dynamics of the organizational response was investigated (Johannessen, 2018). The question addressed was why one of the organizations (the Air Force) had reacted faster than expected to the Libya crises in 2011, while the other (the Police) had reacted slower than expected to the twin terror attacks in Oslo and on Utøya in 2011.

The research found that the experience of fluctuations of time directly influenced the coordinating and organizing capabilities during crises and emergency response. Drawing on insights from complexity research to interpret the internal dynamics of the organizations in question, one of the findings was that there was an important link between organizational structure and the perception of time. People in different sections of the organizations had different experiences of time, which had led them to act in different ways and further influence other people's patterns of action. As the hierarchical structure of the organizations was dependent on the actions and rhythms of people's daily work, it broke down under time pressure and had to be restructured in the form of various networks of people. The way the collapse happened, and the way it was restructured, was dependent on rehearsed perceptions of time, which were different in the two organizations. This could explain the different tempos and reaction times of the operations.

94   *Philosophy, Science, and Organizational Practice*

The Air Force ended up acting too fast in relation to what they were supposed to do because the part of the organization that was mobilized had been trained to react and coordinate fast and to release themselves from bureaucratic restrain. By contrast, the Police had acted too slowly to be able to make sense of what they had to do because different units trained to have different reaction times were involved, while at the same time they were not trained to release themselves from bureaucratic and formal restrictions.

Consequently, in both cases (the Air Force and the Police), the real strategies emerged within the time-space of the organizational structuring of practice, and they did so to a large degree with great difference in leadership activity. These real strategies formed spontaneously, with very short time frames, while formal strategies were formed later as constructions of what had already happened. Such strategies were noted as negative strategies because they were plans about the past, not the future. The different patterns were explainable from previous patterns of training, as it seemed that actors in both organizations had mainly followed their trained patterns instead of changing their patterns to make sense of and respond to the real situation, which clearly was new to their experience.

References

Allen, P.M. (1998). Evolving complexity in social science. In: Altman, G. & Koch, W.A. (eds.) *Systems: New Paradigms for the Human Sciences*, pp. 3–38. Berlin: Walter de Gruyter.
Anderson, P. (1999). Complexity theory and organization science. *Organization Science* 10, pp. 216–232.
Arthur, W.B. (1989). Competing technologies, increasing returns, and lock-in by historical events. *The Economic Journal* 99, pp. 116–131.
Arthur, W.B. (2014). *Complexity and the Economy*. Oxford: Oxford University Press.
Axelrod, R. (1997). *The Complexity of Cooperation: Agent-Based Models for Competition and Collaboration*. Princeton, NJ: Princeton University Press.
Axelrod, R. (2006). *The Evolution of Cooperation*. Revised ed. New York: Basic Books.
Black, J.A. & Farias, G. (2000). Dynamic strategies: Emergent journeys. *Emergence* 2(1), pp. 101–113.
Boje, D.M. (2000). Phenomenal complexity theory and change at Disney: Response to Letiche. *Journal of Organizational Change Management* 3(6), pp. 558–566.
Brown, S.L. & Eisenhardt, K.M. (1998). *Competing on the Edge: Strategy as Structured Chaos*. Boston, MA: Harvard Business School Press.
Byrne, D. (2003). Complexity theory and planning theory: A necessary encounter. *Planning Theory* 2(3), pp. 171–178.

Campbell-Hunt, C. (2007). Complexity in practice. *Human Relations* 60(5), pp. 793–823.

Carlisle, Y. & McMillan, E. (2006). Innovation in organizations from a complex adaptive systems perspective. *Emergence: Complexity and Organization* 8(1), pp. 2–9.

Chettiparamb, A. (2006). Metaphors in complexity theory and planning. *Planning Theory* 5(1), pp. 71–91.

Cunha, M.P. & Cunha, J.V. (2006). Towards a complexity theory of strategy. *Management Decision* 44(7), pp. 839–850.

Eisenhardt, K.M. & Piezunka, H. (2011). Complexity theory and corporate strategy. In: Maguire, S., Allen, D. & McKelvey, B. (eds.) *The SAGE Handbook of Complexity and Management*, pp. 508–525. London: SAGE.

Elias, N. (2000). *The Civilizing Process: Sociogenetic and Psychogenetic Investigations*. Revised ed. Oxford: Blackwell.

Fayol, H. (1949 [1919]). *General and Industrial Management*. London: Pitman.

Ferguson, N. (2010). Complexity and collapse: Empires on the edge of chaos. *Foreign Affairs* March/April, pp. 18–32.

Goldstein, J. (2000). Emergence: A construct amid a thicket of conceptual snares. *Emergence* 2(1), pp. 5–22.

Hodge, B. & Coronado, G. (2007). Understanding change in organizations in a far-from-equilibrium world. *Emergence* 9(3), pp. 3–15.

Johannessen, S.O. (2018). *Strategies, Leadership and Complexity in Crisis and Emergency Operations*. New York: Routledge.

Johannessen, S.O. & Stacey, R.D. (2005). Technology as social object: A complex responsive processes perspective. In: Stacey, R.D. (ed.) *Experiencing Emergence in Organisations: Local Interaction and the Emergence of Global Patterns*, pp. 142–163. London: Routledge.

Levinthal, D.A. (1997). Adaptation on rugged landscapes. *Management Science* 43, pp. 934–950.

Lewin, R. (1992). *Complexity: Life at the Edge of Chaos*. New York: MacMillan.

Lissack, M.R. (1999). Complexity: The science, its vocabulary, and its relation to organizations. *Emergence* 1(1), pp. 110–126.

MacIntosh, R. & MacLean, D. (1999). Conditioned emergence: A dissipative structures approach to transformation. *Strategic Management Journal* 20(4), pp. 297–316.

MacIntoch, R. & MacLean, D. (2001). Conditioned emergence: Researching change and changing research. *International Journal of Operations & Production Management* 21(10), pp. 1343–1357.

Maguire, S. & McKelvey, B. (1999). Complexity and management: Moving from fad to firm foundations. *Emergence* 1(2), pp. 12–61.

McGuiness, T. & Morgan, R.E. (2000). Strategy, dynamic capabilities and complex science: Management rhetoric vs. reality. *Strategic Change* 9(4), pp. 209–220.

McKelvey, B. (1999). Complexity theory in organization science: Seizing the promise or becoming a fad. *Emergence* 1(1), pp. 5–33.

Nilsson, F.R. (2019). A complexity perspective on logistics management: Rethinking assumptions for the sustainability era. *The International Journal of Logistics Management* 30(3), pp. 681–698.

Nonaka, I. & Takeuchi, H. (1995). *The Knowledge Creating Company: How Japanese Companies Create the Dynamics of Innovation.* New York: Oxford University Press.

Penrose, E.T. (1959). *The Theory of the Growth of the Firm.* New York: Wiley.

Prahalad, C.K. & Hamel, G. (1990). The core competence of the corporation. *Harvard Business Review* 68, pp. 78–91.

Raisio, H., Puustinen, A. & Jäntti, J. (2020). The security environment has always been complex: The views of Finnish military officers on complexity. *Defence Studies* 20(4), pp. 390–411.

Sanders, T.I. (1998). *Strategic Thinking and the New Science: Planning in the Midst of Chaos, Complexity, and Change.* New York: Free Press.

Stacey, R. (1995). The science of complexity: An alternative perspective for strategic change processes. *Strategic Management Journal* 16, pp. 477–495.

Stacey, R.D. (2007). *Strategic Management and Organisational Dynamics: The Challenge of Complexity.* 5th ed. London: Pearson Education.

Streatfield, P. (2001). *The Paradox of Control in Organizations.* London: Routledge.

Taylor, F. (1911). *Principles of Scientific Management.* New York: Harper & Bros.

Taylor, J. (2005). Leadership and cult values: Moving from the idealized to the experienced. In: Griffin, D. & Stacey, R.D. (eds.) *Complexity and the Experience of Leading Organizations*, pp. 126–150. London: Routledge.

Weick, K. (1995). *Sensemaking in Organizations.* Thousand Oaks, CA: SAGE.

Zhu, Z. (2007). Complexity science, systems thinking and pragmatic sensibility. *Systems Research & Behavioral Science* 24(4), pp. 445–464.

8 Complexity Ideas in Leadership and Organizational Change

Leadership

Complexity research demonstrates that economic and organizational relations are fundamentally *uncertain* (Arthur, 2014). Unforeseen crises, surprises, and collapse of organizations may emerge and drastically change any plan or structure within short time spans, even if the actors sustain the hierarchies and formal structures (Johannessen, 2018). Such macro results are not generated from underlying linear causes. *Non-linearity* is a necessary precaution for complexity – an unavoidable aspect of organizations. Interactions among people, technologies, and other types of resources lead to complex behaviour, which demands coordination between spontaneous changes and the constraints of the interacting world. The origin of *irreversibility* in organizations is related to complexity in the sense that simultaneous micro-processes and macroscopic manifestations emerge outside the individual actors' sphere of interaction. However, uncertainty cannot be contained and controlled by more information or more advanced systems of control. There are no clear limits or boundaries as to where and how decisions of leaders influence the total evolution of organizations. Emerging properties in organizations manifest themselves through the creation of *self-organized* conditions, in which order and coordination are created through complex interactions between actors operating locally across formal hierarchies.

However, local experiences of organized activity are often neglected and minimized at the expense of abstract control programmes. In systems thinking it is thought that feedback loops and plans are necessary for people to do things successfully, while in complexity thinking successful organizational activity is based on a quality of relating and communication between the people involved. In this sense, attempts to simplify and reduce non-linear reality to linear reality, which is the case with plans and procedures, can only be attempts at simplifying and reducing ways of relating and communicating. Given that organizations are shaped in this dynamic and uncertain way, what could and should leaders be doing?

DOI: 10.4324/9781003042501-10

From the CAS-inspired direction of organizational complexity research, several researchers, among them Uhl-Bien et al. (2007), have argued that in transforming organizations from the industrial age to the knowledge era, new forms of leadership are necessary. In particular, they claim that employees need to have more freedom to create, and less control and fewer hierarchical procedures. Their argument of a complexity leadership theory is built on findings from CAS research regarding how interactions between locally informed agents evolve as larger patterns of action. Furthermore, they argue that in formal bureaucratic organizations, informal leadership behaviour can be important in order to enhance innovation, adaptability, and learning.

In the same stream, Hazy (2011) argues that traditional management research has been unsatisfactory in terms of its practice and that complexity insights would mean five new 'rules of management': *first*, focus on the evolution of organizational resilience and not design for stability; *second*, be open to surprises across all levels of the organization; *third*, create effectiveness by looking forwards (not backwards) and anticipating that the future will be qualitatively different from the present; *fourth*, build models and encourage trial-and-error experimentation; and *fifth*, recognize and reinforce larger-scale patterns to ride a wave of renewal.

MacIntoch and MacLean (1999) used the language of complexity science to argue theoretically that it is possible to manage processes of emergence and self-organization. Their claim was that organizational transformation could be viewed as an emergent process that can be accessed and influenced by order-generating rules, disequilibrium, and positive feedback. However, based on a four-year ethnographic study of a public-sector organization, Houchin and MacLean (2005) argued that simplistic applications of complexity theory to cultural and social settings are inadequate. For complexity theory to be useful to management practice, it has to embrace theories and principles from psychology and social theory. Houchin and MacLean used narratives to describe the development of management practice in terms of four ideas from complexity theory: sensitivity to initial conditions, negative and positive feedback processes, disequilibrium, and emergent order. Their findings led them to question the assertion that organizations are naturally complex adaptive systems that produce novel forms of order. Instead, they proposed an alternative view, that stability-seeking behaviour is the norm in organized human activity and that this then leads to self-organizing hierarchy.

Redefining Top-Down and Bottom-Up

A key issue in organizational change is the tension between a 'top-down leadership' (hierarchical) and 'bottom-up leadership' (democratic) in change processes. Since World War II there has been a broad shift from the individual towards the group in organizational thinking (Johannessen, 2009). This shift has been concurrent with a changed view of effective industrial organization from functional, well-defined, simple working tasks towards more complicated operations being handled by teams. This in turn has led to tensions in the views on top-down and bottom-up leadership. However, by reifying leadership along such spatial dimensions, mainstream literature often punctuates the paradoxical power dynamics of individual and group phenomena. Complexity thinking points to how paradox is inherent in organizational activities and how being aware of this can be helpful for leaders who are trying to understand these processes in their own practice.

In taking this seriously, Nol Groot and John Tobin, both with long-term experience as senior executives of large organizations, in many ways redefined what a top-down and bottom-up approach can mean in practice based on complexity thinking. Groot (2009) explained how his change of practice in the Dutch railways influenced his sense of identity as a leader when acting without the notion of being in control, at the same time as the organization slowly reorganized itself creatively and became more effective in fulfilling its purpose of providing transport to the public. Tobin (2009) wrote about a complex process of merging two hospitals in the United States, and how his role as a CEO in the change process was as a political figure holding this complicated process on track by keeping in touch with a multitude of different intentions, both balancing and confronting them from his position of power. Thus, he attempted to hold the tension of the paradoxical situations of top-down and bottom-up that emerged. Groot and Tobin understood their change of practice with explicit reference to the insights from complexity theories.

Groot and Tobin did not underestimate their formal positions, but they took seriously the influence and responsibility of having been trusted with a different kind of power position than other people in the same organization. At the same time, they took seriously the patterns that emerged between people in their organization, and they developed a practice of trying to relate to and being in touch with the local conversational themes; that is, they took seriously what traditionally is seen as the bottom-up processes of the organization. This, then, became both Groot's and Tobin's everyday effective arenas of negotiating their own intentions and responsibilities in relation to other people's intentions and responsibilities, something that built trust, which turned out to be a constructive route forward for making leadership matter in social negotiation of development and change work.

In their practice of being at 'the top' and having responsibility for large-scale change and development activities, Groot and Tobin found the power issues particularly difficult. Relentlessly over long time periods they had to endure the difficulties that arose in the everyday communicative negotiations. Even if they were seen as powerful figures, they did not experience themselves nearly as powerful as others might have thought. For Groot and Tobin, just as for other people in their respective organizations, change and development was difficult. However, engaging with other groups and people in the hierarchy from their unique positions as senior leaders demanded more of them as leaders, but also turned out to produce better results. They understood that they too had to change their own practice if they were going to succeed in motivating people in their organizations to change their practice. This simple realization seems to be quite rare among top leaders. It is more common for top leaders to demand and command change in their organization without changing anything in their own practice. They act on the grounds that organizations are systems or structures outside their own interaction, structures that they have the power to change as they wish. Complexity thinking implies an interactional, communicative, and dynamic perspective on organizing and change. Hence, in order for organizations to change, patterns of interaction and communication must change, and therefore leaders need to change their own patterns too.

The Role of the Consultant

Leaders often hire consultants to help them in change programmes. Consultation as a practice has traditionally taken different routes, dependent on ideas and understanding in different disciplines. Organizational development and consultation originated as a field just after World War II, as part of the attention towards human relations in organizations (see Chapter 1). It was anchored in psychological approaches, and since the 1940s it has been associated with prominent researchers such as Lewin (1947), Emery and Trist (1960), Argyris and Schön (1978), and Schein (1985). The researchers explored learning and development of individuals, groups, and cultures, including leader groups.

In parallel with the research done in these fields, a consulting industry has emerged based on more or less fancy concepts with no basis in research. Many of the concepts are not meant for use in the context of involvement and exploration of change in organizations, but rather in the context of a hard top-down and entirely detached activity, whereby senior leaders make decisions about abstract restructuring and change in models without any real contact with the people in the organization. Often, this turns out to be a cynical game in which the distance between ordinary employees and the top leaders turns into a 'canyon' of distrust. This instrumental approach is the ghost of Taylorism haunting, in particular, large organizations. Originally, the ideas of organizational development were meant to engage several groups in the organization in long-term development activities. It seems that this has lost much interest among leaders, in favour of the coaching and concept industry. It also implies that there is a wide difference in views of what complexity means in organizational development work. According to the earlier-described new Taylorism, consultation often aims at removing complexity.

Taking complexity thinking as the point of departure would mean to develop further the tradition of research-based organizational development. Christensen (2005) explores this route and argues that the practice of consultation can readily be seen as akin to a research practice, and that the approach or method is one of exploring experience as it emerges between participants in change programmes, whether in business organizations or in the contexts of learning sessions for educational purposes.

However, being explorative is not the same as to operate without intention. The consultant's intentions emerge and are continuously negotiated. Although the consultant often takes responsibility for setting the arenas for exploration and suggesting activities, he or she will also seek to keep open the question of how activities are to progress during conversations. By doing this, the consultant places the responsibility for upholding and potentially changing conversational themes on all participants involved. Based on this, Christensen (2005) terms a complexity approach of both the researcher and the consultant in development activities *emergent participative exploration*.

Innovation

Traditionally, researchers have pointed to innovation as a rational activity necessary for organizations' competition and adaptation in a market (Porter, 1980). Such a view has mainly assumed that innovation happens within existing organizations (Snyder and Duarte, 2003; Koc and Ceylan, 2007). The reference point for innovation is activity that is known. When organizations compete and adapt, it is in constant relation to what others in the same market do (Tidd et al., 2005). However, this does not explain how new businesses emerge (Boisot, 1998; Hamel, 2000).

A different view than the rational one broke through as a result of the new reality of knowledge and information technology (IT). The IT business did not rise from competition or adaptation to existing industries of the 1980s. It was something new, and it has since expanded to become a new dominant practice in virtually every sector of society and economies. Initially, in trying to explain this, researchers thought about spontaneity, resources, and knowledge as possible factors and found support in the economic theories of Schumpeter (1934) and Hayek (1948). These theories are related to evolutionary theory and they refer to the importance of innovating and renewal in organizations as a form of 'survival of the fittest'. Novelty is seen as spontaneous, analogous to genetic mutations in organisms. However, even if spontaneity is a real human experience in the shape and form of fantasy and creativity, there is a big difference between a new idea and a new practice, new product, or a new market. Converting an idea to a profitable production has little to do with spontaneity and much to do with hard work, power struggles, and communication practices (Johannessen and Aasen, 2007). Novelty arising in organizational practices cannot be explained either by the rational choices of leaders or as evolutionary selection. This does not mean that the choices of leaders, good fortune, or timing in a market with a new product are not important; it just means that there is much more going on, which is why complexity becomes the centre of attention.

Innovation was one of the early themes in which researchers saw possibilities for new explanations by drawing on chaos and complexity theories. Some of the references to the language of chaos appeared with Quinn (1985), who suggested that the management of innovation required 'controlled chaos', and with Peters (1987), who prescribed 'thriving on chaos'. In the 1990s, Goldstein (1994) discussed how deviations from routines could be seen as analogous to the fluctuations that Prigogine described as crucial to producing new structures (dissipative structures). Goldstein proposed that to bring about organizational renewal such structures should be amplified rather than dampened.

Researchers in the CAS stream argued that it was necessary to create new frameworks to ease the implementation of some of the complexity-based ideas, notably those relating to learning, innovation, creativity, or, more generally, change (Marion and Uhl-Bien, 2001). One example of this approach can be seen in the work of Surie and Hazy (2006), who proposed a theoretical framework for a special form of leadership that, through relational quality, creates organizational conditions that nurture innovation rather than individual traits of creativity.

Other researchers explored the properties of CAS in order to develop new organizational theories that embraced change as an emergent self-organizing process rather than as orderly controllable steps (Anderson, 1999; Price, 2004). This approach has led to new knowledge about innovation processes and the management of innovation (Poole and Van de Ven, 2004; Frenken, 2005, 2006; Carlisle and McMillan, 2006; van Buuren and Edelenbos, 2006). Many of the new contributions merged empirical observation with computational agent-based simulation, demonstrating non-linear and self-organizing systems behaviour.

However, computer simulations were criticized as being unable to capture the full range of human experience and of falling short in taking seriously emotional responses, power relations, identity, and unconscious group processes, all of which are very important phenomena in organizations (Stacey,

2003). Such processes serve to include persons, ideas, and behaviours adhering to established patterns of action and to exclude persons who represent patterns of action that are new or different (Elias and Scotson, 1994; Dalal, 1998), insights that clearly are relevant to the understanding of processes of innovation.

By showing the importance of misunderstandings in creating new solutions in organizations, Fonseca (2001) provided a good empirical example of how the human reality of innovation processes cannot be captured by computer simulations. Misunderstandings can be described in complexity terms as bifurcation points, where the trajectory of history suddenly takes one surprising course instead of another one that was expected. However, even if bifurcation points could be simulated by a computer, they would not make any organizational or human sense without understanding what they represent or how they come about in terms of human practice and experience. By demonstrating how misunderstandings are important in innovation, Fonseca was able to point to the crucial importance of communication practices for innovation and at the same time show that surprises with unpredictable consequences are common features of such practices.

Thus, it is of limited value to analyse innovation processes and organizational capacity for innovation without taking into consideration the communicative nature of organizations, and how communication shapes power relations, identity, and the emergence of new meaning in organizational contexts.

Innovation as Communication

Based on a longitudinal ethnographic study of a technology research community in a large international energy company, Aasen and Johannessen (2007, 2009) highlighted the communicative nature of organizations in innovation processes and demonstrated how complexity thinking can bring new insights into what is going on when people are innovating in organizations. This type of research directs attention towards the self-organizing patterning processes of local communicative interaction. Self-organization takes the form of co-evolving repetitive and transformative patterning of communicative themes that are created when people interact and talk with each other. In this sense, innovation is seen as self-organizing, emergent, and irreversible patterning of new themes of communication. When a new theme emerges and becomes iterated and incorporated in the conversations between members of the organization, it also contributes to the patterning of a new organizational identity or structure, while at the same time other patterns fade into the background as part of the organization's identity history.

When innovation is talked about in organizations, it is as a global and general theme that appears in the conversations of many people. Simultaneously, in the context of a group meeting, the question arises as to what the themes of innovation might mean for the group. Such discussions are influenced by the relationships between the members of or participants in the group and the quality of their relating, in which power is always an experience. Therefore, power relations contribute to the wider patterns of interaction between people. The generalized pattern and the local particularized interactions happen at the same time, and it is not possible to identify which comes before the other. These aspects of patterning – the global and the local – cannot be separated from each other because wider organizational patterns are always enacted locally. When patterns are playing out, individuals are expressing both their individual identity themes (particularities) and the global identity themes (generality) at the same time. As they are expressing this, they are contributing to the emergence of both local meaning and further generalization of themes and actions. They are simultaneously globalizing as they are particularizing and vice versa.

Seen in the way described in the preceding section, innovation is not a rationally planned process, nor is it an evolutionary process driven by chance or selection mechanisms. Rather, it is the result of a number of activities that are closely integrated in everyday life into organizations (Johannessen and Aasen, 2007). Organized activity consists of an infinite number of local conversations and interactions in which many individuals create, express, and respond to local and global communicative themes. Certain individuals (leaders) are meant to influence the communicative themes more than others should. However, the influencers are not always formal leaders. As a top-down process, innovation is seen as a hierarchical phenomenon in which communicative patterns are implemented according to a strategic plan in such a way that a particular type of innovative behaviour emerges (see Chapter 7). Top leaders can influence what people in an organization are doing by increasing, removing, or allocating resources. However, bottom-up processes, which seek to include ordinary employees in the strategic innovation processes, are also important in order to create an innovation culture. In a similar manner as change processes in organizations, leaders who change their practice and move beyond the dichotomy of top-down and bottom-up might increase their chances of succeeding also with innovation processes (Groot, 2009; Tobin, 2009). It was clearly demonstrated in the study of Aasen and Johannessen (2007) that the everyday practices of leaders had a decisive importance on the people who were tasked with inventing new solutions to very challenging problems.

Power, Identity, and Values

Ongoing power struggles are an important feature of organized activity and as such they are relevant to innovation processes. As projects progress, conflicting interests, as well as cooperation, support, and counteractivity emerge. Thus, organizations can be seen as power – identity structures causing various coexisting communicational themes to emerge, resulting in differences in the purpose and importance of particular activities. In many organizations, there are two hierarchies, one expert and one operational hierarchy. Experts might promote new ideas and solutions, but they might also argue against new ideas. Thus, influential individuals could suppress new themes while also being empowered to legitimize new themes of communication. Sometimes resistance is sound, but it can also be about sustaining existing power identities. If a company moves from one type of business to another, new solutions could leave existing experts less influential. Lack of support from experts could then be related to potential shifts of power relations and identities, and as such to changed patterns of interaction. New ideas are new themes of communication, which in turn are organizing experiences of power and identity in new ways.

Therefore, innovation projects are ongoing power identity-forming processes that are shaped by various interests, while at the same time shaping and transforming the interests of individuals who in some way are engaged in the activities. New ideas emerge from a multitude of conversations that represent challenges, change, acknowledgement, and rejection. When innovation is materialized in new technology or experienced as new practice, it is the experience of new generalized patterns of action (Johannessen and Stacey, 2005). Additionally, the processes of communicative interaction and power-relating may take the form of idealizations or cult values (Griffin, 2002). Such cult values have the effect of including those who adhere to them and excluding those who do not, thereby establishing collective 'we' identities for all individuals in both groupings (Dalal, 1998). Thus, cult values both enable and constrain the actors at the same time and as such can be seen as the foundation of humans' ability to coordinate. Such descriptions make it possible to provide new explanations of the most fundamental organizational theme of coordination.

Innovation can be one such formulation of a cult value and thus a foundation for a new coordinating pattern. The practising of the cult value of innovation inevitably leads to both the conflict (instability) and the negotiation of compromises around such conflict (stability). Innovation is enacted in the ordinary local interactions between people. Such enactment both produces and is produced from stability and instability in communication themes.

106   *Philosophy, Science, and Organizational Practice*

Aasen and Johannessen (2007) argue in favour of the value and potential of shifting the focus of attention in research on complexity and innovation in organizations towards exploring the basic feature of organizational life, which is communicative interaction (Mead, 1977 [1934]). Reproduction and transformation of phenomena such as power and identity are essential and imply the need for research on how innovation emerges from the experiences of everyday organizational life. Thus, organizational practices are the key focuses for research on complexity and change in organizations.

References

Aasen, T.M. & Johannessen, S. (2007). Exploring innovation processes from a complexity perspective. Part II: Experiences from the SIOR case. *International Journal of Learning and Change* 2(4), pp. 434–446.
Aasen, T.M. & Johannessen, S. (2009). Managing innovation as communicative processes: A case of subsea technology R&D. *International Journal of Business Science and Applied Management* 4(3), pp. 22–33.
Anderson, P. (1999). Complexity theory and organization science. *Organization Science* 10, pp. 216–232.
Argyris, C. & Schön, D. (1978). *Organizational Learning: A Theory of Action Perspective*. Reading, MA: Addison-Wesley.
Arthur, W.B. (2014). *Complexity and the Economy*. Oxford: Oxford University Press.
Boisot, M. (1998). *Knowledge Assets: Securing Competitive Advantage in the Knowledge Economy*. Oxford: Oxford University Press.
Carlisle, Y. & McMillan, E. (2006). Innovation in organizations from a complex adaptive systems perspective. *Emergence: Complexity and Organization* 8(1), pp. 2–9.
Christensen, B.B. (2005). Emerging participative exploration: Consultation as research. In: Stacey, R.D. & Griffin, D. (eds.) *A Complexity Perspective on Researching Organizations: Taking Experience Seriously*, pp. 78–106. London: Routledge.
Dalal, F. (1998). *Taking the Group Seriously: Towards a Post-Foulkesian Group Analytic Theory*. London: Jessica Kingsley.
Elias, N. & Scotson, J.L. (1994). *The Established and the Outsiders: A Sociological Enquiry into Community Problems*. London: SAGE.
Emery, F.E. & Trist, E.L. (1960). *Socio-Technical Systems in Management Science: Models and Techniques*. Oxford: Pergamon Press.
Fonseca, J. (2001). *Complexity and Innovation in Organisations*. London: Routledge.
Frenken, K. (2005). *Innovation, Evolution and Complexity Theory*. Cheltenham: Edward Elgar.
Frenken, K. (2006). Technological innovation and complexity theory. *Economics of Innovation and New Technology* 15, pp. 137–155.

Goldstein, J. (1994). *The Unshackled Organization*. Portland, OR: Productivity Press.

Griffin, D. (2002). *The Emergence of Leadership: Linking Self-Organization and Ethics*. London: Routledge.

Groot, N. (2009). Senior executives and the emergence of local responsibilities: A complexity approach to identity development and performance improvement. *International Journal of Learning and Change* 3(3), pp. 264–280.

Hamel, G. (2000). *Leading the Revolution*. Boston, MA: Harvard Business School Press.

Hayek, F.A. (1948). *Individualism and Economic Order*. London: Routledge.

Hazy, J.K. (2011). Parsing the 'influential increment' in the language of complexity: Uncovering the systemic mechanisms of leadership influence. *International Journal of Complexity in Leadership and Management* 1(3), pp. 3–20.

Houchin, K. & MacLean, D. (2005). Complexity theory and strategic change: An empirically informed critique. *British Journal of Management* 16(2), pp. 149–166.

Johannessen, S.O. (2009). The complexity turn in studies of organisations and leadership: Relevance and implications. *International Journal of Learning and Change* 3(3), pp. 214–229.

Johannessen, S.O. (2018). *Strategies, Leadership and Complexity in Crisis and Emergency Operations*. New York: Routledge.

Johannessen, S.O. & Aasen, T.M.B. (2007). Exploring innovation processes from a complexity perspective. Part I: Theoretical and methodological approach. *International Journal of Learning and Change* 2(4), pp. 420–433.

Johannessen, S.O. & Stacey, R.D. (2005). Technology as social object: A complex responsive processes perspective. In: Stacey, R.D. (ed.) *Experiencing Emergence in Organisations: Local Interaction and the Emergence of Global Patterns*, pp. 142–163. London: Routledge.

Koc, T. & Ceylan, C. (2007). Factors impacting the innovative capacity in large-scale companies. *Technovation* 27, pp. 105–114.

Lewin, K. (1947). Frontiers in group dynamics: Concept, method and reality in social science: Social equilibrium and social change. *Human Relations* 1(1), pp. 5–41.

MacIntoch, R. & MacLean, D. (1999). Conditioned emergence: Researching change and changing research. *International Journal of Operations and Production Management* 21, pp. 1343–1357.

Marion, R. & Uhl-Bien, M. (2001). Leadership in complex organizations. *Leadership Quarterly* 12(4), pp. 389–418.

Mead, G.H. (1977 [1934]). *Mind, Self and Society*. Edited and introduced by Charles W. Morris. Chicago: Chicago University Press.

Peters, T. (1987). *Thriving on Chaos: Handbook for a Management Revolution*. London: Macmillan.

Poole, M.S. & Van de Ven, A.H. (2004). *Handbook of Organizational Change and Innovation*. New York: Oxford University Press.

Porter, M.E. (1980). *Competitive Strategy: Techniques for Analyzing Industries and Competitors*. New York: Free Press.

Price, I. (2004). Complexity, complicatedness and complexity: A new science behind organizational intervention? *Emergence: Complexity and Organization* 6(1–2), pp. 40–48.

Quinn, J.B. (1985). Managing innovation: Controlled chaos. *Harvard Business Review* 63(3), pp. 73–84.

Schein, E.H. (1985). *Organizational Culture and Leadership*. San Francisco, CA: Jossey-Bass.

Schumpeter, J.A. (1934). *The Theory of Economic Development*. New York: Oxford University Press.

Snyder, N.T. & Duarte, D.L. (2003). *Strategic Innovation: Embedding Innovation as a Core Competency in Your Organization*. San Francisco, CA: Jossey-Bass.

Stacey, R.D. (2003). *Complexity and Group Processes: A Radically Social Understanding of Individuals*. London: Brunner-Routledge.

Surie, G. & Hazy, J.K. (2006). Generative leadership: Nurturing innovation in complex systems. *Emergence: Complexity and Organization* 8(4), pp. 13–26.

Tidd, J., Bessant, J. & Pavitt, K. (2005). *Managing Innovation: Integrating Technological, Market and Organizational Change*. 3rd ed. Chichester: Wiley and Sons.

Tobin, J. (2009). The myth of rational objectivity and leadership: The realities of a hospital merger from a CEO's perspective. *International Journal of Learning and Change* 3(3), pp. 248–263.

Uhl-Bien, M., Marion, R. & McKelvey, B. (2007). Complexity leadership theory: Shifting leadership from the industrial age to the knowledge era. *Leadership Quarterly* 18, pp. 298–318.

van Buuren, A. & Edelenbos, J. (2006). Innovations in the Dutch polder: Communities of practice and the challenge of coevolution. *Emergence: Complexity and Organization* 8(1), pp. 42–49.

Epilogue

The human condition is immersed in crises, conflict, and radical changes in nature, technology, economy, politics, and society. Large-scale changes in the earth's climate and biosphere threaten natural life and human societies around the world. Wars continue to rage, terrorism sees no borders between countries, while poverty and hunger disasters still are a reality for millions of people. In 2020, the COVID-19 brought about a global crisis that led to millions of deaths and a worldwide economic shock, the scale of which has hardly ever been witnessed before. Even in countries with highly developed democracies and health services, death tolls were catastrophically high.

In some countries, the consequences of the disease seemed to be amplified by the lack of political leadership and scientific advice. By contrast, in other countries the consequences seemed to be prolonged by people's lack of trust in political leadership and scientific advice. Although the pandemic was curbed by unprecedented scientific efforts to develop and roll-out efficient and safe vaccines rapidly, which saved millions of lives, many people refused to be vaccinated.

Despite many global crises, in general terms, great progress is being made within science, medicine, and 'green' technologies. Research, company strategies, public awareness, and government policies clearly aim at dealing with existential challenges and improve the quality and sustainability of our planet. A larger portion than ever before of the world's population enjoy democracy, education, health care, and lives without poverty. According to the United Nations, the number of people living in extreme poverty declined from 36 per cent in 1990 to 10 per cent in 2015, even if in the same period the world's population increased with billions of people. However, this also means that more than 700 million people still live in extreme poverty. Additionally, the economic fallout in the wake of the pandemic has threatened to increase the percentage of people living in extreme poverty for the first time in 30 years. Even though modernity carries an intrinsic promise that the natural and engineering sciences, enlightened democracy, and economic growth are supposed to create a more stable, certain, rational, predictable, and controlled world, it seems that nature and society are not behaving in accordance with the established world view of the natural and social sciences. Science has no grand formula for reality. Hence, our challenge is to ask new and fundamental questions about the dynamics of nature and society, questions that can vitalize new ways of thinking, understanding, and responding to uncertainty and surprises.

We live in a world of complexity. While flow of information on the Internet and in social media is making freedom of expression easier, the rules of law and human rights are challenged daily, even in highly advanced democracies, as surveillance, state control, and fake news are whirling around in a truly worldwide web of information. Technological control is masked and diluted by euphoric and voluntary illusions of freedom that are reminiscent of Aldous Huxley's 1932 science fiction novel *Brave New World*. In the novel, control of society is made real by substituting citizens' political and social awareness with the superficial happiness derived from indulging in shopping and drugs.

We are openly and consciously moving into *virtual reality*, beyond any distinction that once seemed clear-cut between the sciences of reality and the fictions of the future. While the term *cybernetics* initially alluded to a rational science by which humans could control technology, it soon morphed into a new utopia of 'Thinking Machines' and artificial intelligence – in which technology control humans. William Gibson's 1984 science fiction novel *Neuromancer*, which first coined the term *cyberspace* and described it as *unthinkable complexity*, pointed towards our present-day reality. However, today's chaotic and blurred virtual social reality has spiralled into a trajectory beyond even fiction writers' imagination.

As we have come to enter this brave new world of cyberspace and unthinkable complexity, the idea of freedom seems to be a peculiar paradox. Control in organizations and society is often characterized by a purpose of *reducing* complexity by means of technology and management systems. However, the realities and challenges of business and society demand creativity, innovation, and dynamic strategies of change – processes that create *increased* complexity. Additionally, in liberal and democratic societies, human freedom means that everyone has a right to pursue their hopes, ambitions, and dreams within the framework of humane laws. On a global scale, such open societies produce an infinite number of interactions between people, technology, and the natural world, which further increases complexity and reduces control. However, as we effortless and seemingly freely scan all directions and dimensions of the highly interactive and dynamic network of information and communication created and enabled by the Internet and all types of mobile and smart devices that are continuing to be integrated into our lives, we also seem willing to give up our freedom by voluntarily carrying surveillance equipment around with us.

The contrast between technological control and human freedom and imagination is one way of expressing the call to take seriously complexity in organizations. From early 20th-century Taylorism, through 1950s cybernetics, and up to present-day global networks, artificial intelligence, and big data, the idea that the natural and social world is controllable through technological simplification and standardization constitutes a large historical river of thought, along which organizational ideas continue to flow. It seems that the ghost of Taylorism has morphed, mutated, and adapted itself throughout time, only to confront us with the enduring conundrum of modernity: can uncertainty, unpredictability, and complexity in nature and society be understood and dealt with by the sciences of certainty and the ideologies of control?

The traditional answer to this question is affirmative, but complexity research clearly rejects this answer. Even if the products of linear thinking and control are entertained and implemented in organizations and societies, there is no escape from complexity. Given our highly dynamic and interactive world, in which humans, technology, and nature are entangled in time, space, and a common destiny, the exploration of complexity cannot be sustained by a rationale of splitting reality into narrow scientific disciplines. On the contrary, investigating complexity is tantamount to taking seriously the interactional, dynamic, and integrative aspects of human, technological, and natural reality. Complexity in human organizing is a consequence of human interaction and a basic feature emerging from the ongoing trade-off and dynamics between the forces, freedom, and constraints of humans, technology, and nature.

Thus, there is every reason to believe that complexity will continue to be at the centre of attention in human affairs. It is from such realization that we should continue to pursue and explore critically and reflexively future research questions about the meaning of complexity in organizations.

Index

identity 78; organizational actors 91;
time-space 83
experiences 75; integrated 91; making
sense of 33
experiences of what one should or
should not do 78

far-from-equilibrium conditions
40–42
feedback and error correction 19
feedback loops 20; cybernetic 19, 22,
24, 65; positive and negative 23–24,
30–31, 37, 65, 98; systems thinking's
perspective on 97
'Feedback Mechanisms...' (Macy
conference) 18
Feigenbaum, Mitchell J. 46
Ferguson, Niall 93
flux 7
flux equilibrium 8
Follett, Mary Parker 5
Fonseca, José 103
Ford factories 4
Ford Foundation 27
Forrester, Jay 29–31; *see also* systems
dynamics
Führerprinzip 11
future organized past, hope for 81
future reality 80–81
fuzziness 33–34

Gadamer, Hans-Georg 61; *Truth and
Method* 63
game theory 17, 18
'generalized other, the' 76
generalized patterns 77
general systemology 11, 22
general systems approach 17
general systems theory 8, 12–14,
22, 29, 48; Bertalanffy's version
of 62
general systems thinking 32; Cillier's
alignment with 73
Germany 5, *see also* Nazi Germany
Gestaltheit 8
Gestalt psychology 9, 19–20
Gibson, William 110
Giddens, Anthony 64
Gleick, James 45; *Chaos* 46–47
Goldstein, Jeffrey 102

Groot, Nol 99–100
group behavior 33–35
group dynamics 23

Habermas, Jürgen 63–67
Habermas–Luhmann debate 65–67
Havel, Vaclav 79
Hayek, Frederick 12, 101
Hazy, J.K. 98, 102
Hawthorne studies 4–5
Heidegger, Martin 61, 67; *Being and
Time* 61, 63
Heims, Steve J. 18, 27
Heisenberg, Werner 42
hermeneutics 61, 66
hierarchization, principle of 8–9
Himmler, Heinrich 12
Hiroshima, bombing of 5, 7
Hitler, Adolf 11
holism 8, 11
holistic systems 7, 10
holistic systems theory 32, 61, 65–67,
72
Holocaust, the 5, 78
homeostatic processes 20
homeostasis 20
homeostat, the 20–21
Houchin, K. 98
human action 69; dual causality
principle guiding 60; Kant's views
on 59–60
human agency 34
human behaviour 78; in organizations
23
human body 20
human brain 20, 82
human complexity: rebuilding 6;
WWII's destruction of 5–8
human condition, the 14, 68, 79, 109
human conflict 81
human creativity 69
human experience: importance of 14;
spontaneity as 102
human freedom 111
human identity 19
human interaction: Stacey's views on
50–51
human issues: computers and science
fused with 29
human morality 78

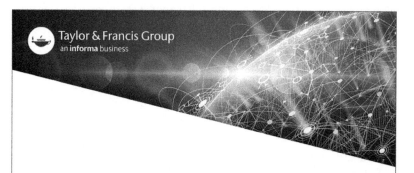

CPSIA information can be obtained
at www.ICGtesting.com
Printed in the USA
BVHW052316020522
635340BV00002B/33

9 780367 860189